Marcus Gill is a dynami~
His knowledge of ''
tive and relevant   ..nany.
His message of faitl.   ..stiny to leave
each person under t.   .~ voice better than they
were before! He is st. ~.cally aligning kingdom leaders
and followers of Christ to take their walk with God to
another level. He's been such a blessing to my ministry and
me, and his teachings still resonate with my congregation.

—BISHOP CHARLES MELLETTE
SENIOR PASTOR, CHRISTIAN PROVISION MINISTRIES
SANFORD, NORTH CAROLINA

Faith Church fell in love with Marcus instantly. He's an
outstanding communicator of the Word, and he has a
sound that can reach every listener. I truly believe that he's
got next in the kingdom. His ministry is groundbreaking,
and his messages are sure to change millions of lives all
around the world.

—FRANK SANTORA
LEAD PASTOR, FAITH CHURCH
NEW MILFORD, CONNECTICUT

Marcus Gill is a prophetic trendsetter to this millennial
generation. His revelation of grace inspires the nations of
the world to love God more and live better lives.

—PROPHET JOSEPH FOSTER
HOST, TCT NETWORK

EVERYBODY WANTS TO WIN

BUT NOBODY WANTS TO WAIT //

MARCUS GILL

 CHARISMA HOUSE

Cover design by Studio Gearbox
Design Director: Justin Evans

Visit the author's website at www.marcusgillinternational.org.

Library of Congress Cataloging-in-Publication Data:
An application to register this book for cataloging has been submitted to the Library of Congress.
International Standard Book Number: 978-1-62999-151-1
E-book ISBN: 978-1-62999-152-8

17 18 19 20 21 — 9 8 7 6 5 4 3 2 1
Printed in the United States of America

To my family, friends, and everyone who has acknowledged appreciation for my inspirational content shared on social media, sthank you.

Contents

Introduction

ARE WE THERE YET?

WAITING IS SO hard! But in one way or another, we are all waiting. Whether we seem to have it all or have the weight of the world on our shoulders, we're all waiting for something—waiting for change, waiting for answers, waiting for healing, waiting for things to get better. No matter how good life gets, every living human being—rich or poor—will always need something.

The troubling thing about having a need is not just wondering *if* the need can be met; it's not knowing *when* the need will be met. Most of us don't go through life wondering *if* we will eat or *if* we will sleep. We go through life wondering *when* we will eat and *when* we will sleep.

Have you ever heard of the "five Ws and one H"—who, what, when where, why, and how? Usually used by journalists as they write newspaper or magazine articles, these are the same questions that bring almost every human to their knees, seeking God for answers. When we need answers in any area of our lives, we want to know who is going to answer us, what the answer will be, where the answer is coming from, why we had to face the challenge in the first place, and how to make sense of everything we're going through. But our biggest question is *when* the answer is coming. Of the six curiosity pushers, the when produces the most anxiety.

We want to know when our answers are coming. Sure, we want what we want right when we want it. However, I believe that if we knew the time and date our answer was coming, we might be able to wait for it. Waiting gets hard when times and circumstances are unpredictable, when things don't happen on our terms or according to our timing. Not knowing when can take out even the strongest, most positive of us.

Delayed Does Not Mean Denied

Having to wait doesn't mean your need will never be met; it just means your answer is delayed. This reminds me of some of my travel experiences.

Some time ago my team members and I were scheduled to return to New York from an amazing singles conference in Jacksonville, Florida. After the conference we made our way back to the airport to board our plane that was scheduled to depart at 8:19 p.m. This was the best time for us to leave on a Saturday, since we wanted to be back early enough to rest before Sunday morning service the next day. The flight was scheduled to be just two hours and forty-five minutes. We knew this flight would allow us to get home in perfect time to lay our heads down and get some rest before the Sunday morning service.

We boarded the plane at 7:55 p.m., found our seats, got

comfortable, and before we knew it, the captain came on the intercom and announced that we would be delayed for twenty minutes. As frustrating as a flight delay can be, twenty minutes wasn't so bad. We patiently waited. But then twenty minutes turned into thirty, and we still hadn't departed. The captain came on again and said that we were now delayed by a whole hour and all the passengers needed to exit the aircraft and wait in the assigned terminal. By that time I was upset.

When we all finally got to the terminal, we heard the gate agent announce that the flight might be canceled and rebooking was an option. I, along with seventy-eight other passengers, was frustrated.

Now, let me paint a picture for you. The other passengers and I knew that our destinations existed. We knew there was a plane available for us to fly on. We knew there were pilots willing and ready to fly us. Our tickets were paid in full, so we shouldn't have had any worry, right? So what was our issue? We didn't know when we were getting to our destinations. We needed answers. We knew who—the airline. We knew what—an airplane. We knew where—New York City. We knew how—flying. What we didn't know was when—the most frustrating question in that whole scenario.

We were told twenty minutes, then an hour, and then that the flight might be canceled. But I learned a lesson through this experience. The airline representatives never said the flight was canceled for sure. They said it might be. So the answer wasn't denied; it was just delayed.

Let God Control Your When

Here's my question to you: Are you living life frustrated because you feel as though the answers you need have been denied? If so, I want to help change your perspective. I want you to understand that it's time for you to get free from trying to control your moments. Stop trying to control your change. Stop trying to control your answers in life.

I got frustrated in the airport because I had no control over when my plane would leave. I had a problem waiting. Had I become so angry and impatient that I left the airport or even rebooked for a later flight, I would have responded inappropriately to a temporary situation and missed out on the opportunity to fly home that same night. What we didn't know was that the flight wasn't going to be canceled and that, soon after a two-hour delay, we would be back on board to fly home to New York. We'd still have enough time to rest up and be ready for a great church service the next day.

What if you chose to be patient and wait just a little while longer? What if you learned how to trust God with your when?

Just as the airline agents served as the authority in that situation at the airport and had control over when we would depart, God has authority and control over your life. He is in control. God knows the who, what, when, where, why, and how for your life. There's no question that God can't answer. There is no sickness He can't heal. There's no debt that He cannot pay. Nothing is impossible with God! It's the negative spirit of impatience and control that makes it hard for us to wait. This is why it's so important that we pray as David did in Psalm 51:10 and ask God to create in us a clean heart and renew the right spirit on the inside. Having the right spirit about life means that we have the right attitude about God's timing being perfect and the humble understanding that we don't control God.

Let God be the one in control. After all, He knows what's best for you.

THERE'S A BLESSING IN WAITING PATIENTLY

Waiting isn't a curse. It's a blessing. Patience is a gift from God. Your life would be so much more joyful if you learned how to wait with patience. King David said in Psalm 40:1–4:

> I waited patiently for the LORD, and He turned to me, and heard my cry. He also brought me up out of a horrible pit, out of the miry clay, and set my feet on a rock, and established my steps. He has put a new song in my mouth, even praise to our God; many will see it, and fear, and will trust in the LORD. Blessed is the man who places trust in the LORD.

A few chapters earlier he said:

> Wait on the LORD; be strong, and may your heart be stout; wait on the LORD.
> —PSALM 27:14

When you wait patiently on the Lord, you gain access to His ear. God hears the prayers of those who wait patiently for Him. When you wait on the Lord, He will come to your rescue. He will deliver you to safety. When you wait patiently on the Lord, your worship will go to a whole new level. When you wait patiently on the Lord, people will see what He has done for you. Your time of waiting will turn into a testimony, and all who witness your deliverance will come to fear and trust in the Lord. When you wait patiently on the Lord, you will be blessed and your heart will be strengthened. Your patient waiting shows God that you trust Him with your whole life, and He rewards faith like that in big ways. Listen, you can't tell me that waiting on God isn't worth it.

Let me challenge you. As you dive deeper into this book, into the blessings that come from waiting patiently on the Lord, I want you to prepare your heart to begin to wait, knowing that God is going to take care of you. Get ready to understand what it really means to trust God with your when.

> When you trust God with your when, you can't help but win.

As I said earlier, we are all in the same boat when it comes to waiting. We all need something. We can also all be in the same boat of victory, if we learn that waiting is always worth it.

If you've previously testified to having a struggle with waiting, my prayer for you is that your perspective on why you're waiting will change. Don't see the answer to your prayer as denied; believe that it's only delayed. Delayed means that something has been released and is on the way, and at that perfect time—on God's clock—you'll be able to celebrate your answer's arrival.

Many of us have such a hard time waiting on God because we haven't asked Him to give us that characteristic of the fruit of the Spirit called longsuffering. Join me in prayer right now to ask God to give you this gift:

> *Father, I thank You for this time in my life. I pray that You would give me limitless strength to endure this waiting season. I don't want to live without Your anointing for longsuffering. I pray that You will empower me to wait on You with a joyful heart, knowing that Your best is being prepared for me right now. Thank You for causing me to win because I choose to trust You. In the name of Jesus I pray, amen.*

Don't get discouraged during your waiting season. God has a plan to bless you in His perfect timing. The blessing may not look the way you thought it would or come the way you expected, but it will be just what you need. Don't quit! God has a miracle with your name on it—and it's worth the wait.

PART I

HOW TO WIN AT THE
WAITING GAME

Chapter 1

IT'S ALL ABOUT TRUST

MOST OF THE pain we face in life is pain others inflict on us. That pain is hard to escape, especially when it's due to the fact that at some point in time we trusted somebody. We don't always know how trust is going to end. We assume when we trust people that they are going to treat us right. Sadly that's not always the case.

If you're honest, you would testify that there have been times in your life when you trusted somebody and that person let you down. It's a joy when you finally meet a person who will not fail you. Yet, more often than we would expect, we discover that people cannot be trusted— or at least trusted on the same level that we trust God.

What is trust? When you trust someone or something, it means you believe that person or thing is reliable, good, honest, or effective. The Bible tells us in Proverbs 3:5–6 to "trust in the LORD with all your heart, and lean not on your own understanding; in all your ways acknowledge

Him, and He will direct your paths." This is one of the most exciting scriptures in the Bible because it gives us instructions on how our paths will be made perfect. It gives us the biggest hint on how to avoid the pitfalls of life.

The reason most of us fail at acknowledging the power in God's timing is that we trust in our own timing and refuse to trust in God's timing. Wouldn't it be much easier for those of us who say we believe in God to truly believe in Him *and* all His ways? The Bible tells us in Psalm 145:17, "The LORD is righteous in all His ways and loving in all His works." We know this! Yet we try to make things happen when we want them to happen because we trust our own instincts. This is a big problem for all of us.

Yes, our feelings are real, but our feelings don't override God's infinite wisdom. The best choice we can make is to trust in God and God alone. I refuse to be the person who misses out on the opportunities God has given me to be blessed beyond measure because I choose to do things the way I want to do them. Yes, everybody wants to win. I want to win. You want to win. There's nothing wrong with having a desire to win or have the victory in Christ Jesus. But one thing we have to do is learn to trust God and His plan for our lives.

It's a waste of time trying to make things happen on your own. Do not waste your energy trying to be God, plain and simple. You must stop trying to be in control of your own life and destiny.

GOD KNOWS YOU BETTER THAN YOU KNOW YOURSELF

Before you were formed in your mother's womb God already had a plan for your life. God already knew how you would look, how you would live, and how you would be successful. He already knew the struggles you would face. He knew you would be reading this book right now even before you were born.

What's my point? I want to get you to understand that trusting God is the best decision you could ever make in life. He knows everything. Why not trust in the One who knows it all? Why trust in yourself when your knowledge is limited? Isn't He the unlimited one? Doesn't He have all power in His hands? Jesus said in Matthew 28:18, "All authority [power in the KJV] has been given to Me in heaven and on earth." So anybody in their right mind who wants to make the right decisions would trust in the One who knows every correct decision to be made.

You know, when we trust in man's words, we can feel good for the moment, but man's words don't last forever. Man's words will give us temporary satisfaction; God's Word will give us everlasting satisfaction.

> People are like grass; their beauty is like a flower in the field. The grass withers and the flower fades. But the word of the Lord remains forever.
> —1 PETER 1:24–25, NLT

Which one would you prefer—a temporary or an everlasting joy? I want to encourage you to choose everlasting joy—a joy that never fades, a joy that remains forever.

I want to motivate you to trust God: He will not fail you. I know that's hard sometimes, but hard things are always worth pushing through. It's going to be better for you in the end if you deal with how hard it may be now rather than trying to take shortcuts to make your journey easy. Trust in the One who makes hard things easy.

> My yoke is easy, and My burden is light.
>
> —MATTHEW 11:30

> Behold, I am the LORD, the God of all flesh. Is anything too hard for Me?
>
> —JEREMIAH 32:27

YOUR TRUST FORECAST

Our ability to trust has a lot to do with what we choose to predict or believe about the future. What type of predictions have you made concerning your life? Are you predicting the right things? Are you planning for the right things based upon your predictions? This is something that we don't think about often. Trust has a lot to do with what we prepare for. We only prepare for what we believe is going to happen.

You're reading this book right now with plans for the future. Even as I speak to you through this book, on some level you're looking forward to things getting better. You may have been down for a while, but your hope, deep down, is that things will start to look up. You should not be in this waiting season expecting things to get worse. You should expect things to get better. When we know that God has good plans for our future (Jer. 29:11) and that He's working things together for our good (Rom. 8:28), it is easy to trust God, because we know what He can do for our future. What makes trust difficult is when we doubt that the things we're believing Him for will actually come to pass.

I've learned this in my lifetime. Trusting God for the future is a sign of faith. It takes great faith to trust God for things that haven't happened yet. Do you have this kind of faith? Can you trust God for things that He hasn't finished yet? If you can answer yes, then you, my friend, have great faith! It's a joy to be able to trust God with the future—to *know* He's going to work a miracle, send financial increase, or heal your body. I trust God with my future. Do you?

Jesus told us to seek first the kingdom of God and all His righteousness, then all these things would be added to us! (See Matthew 6:33.) That's a reason for us to rejoice. Believe this: Tomorrow is full of blessings. Tomorrow is full of change. God has great things in store for us, so why not trust Him?

I choose to trust God. I choose to depend on Him. According to the Word of God, God is able to do exceedingly abundantly above all we can ask or think according to the power that works in us (Eph. 3:20). Because I know God's character and His Word, I know that God will move on my behalf and on your behalf. There's no doubt in my mind.

Receive this now! The Lord is in your life. You can trust that His present and future actions are working in your favor.

He is God all by Himself, and He cannot fail! Because I know that God can't fail, I am confident that He's working things out for my benefit. That makes me excited. I can trust that God will move on my behalf.

The Lord is in my life, and I can trust His present and future actions. We can't always predict what man is going to do, but because of what He has said in His Word, we can know what God is going to do. We don't always understand the plan He has for our future, but one thing we can understand is that the plans are good and not evil. Get ready. Prepare yourself to see the future while you're waiting now. Being able to trust God because of who He is and what He has promised in His Word helps us to relax while waiting today as we prepare for tomorrow.

WHAT WILL YOU GET BACK?

When we put our trust in God, we can expect to receive from Him something far greater than we could have imagined. But trusting God is sometimes easier said than done. Putting our trust into practice can be hard. Even when we know all things are possible with God, we may still question whether He is really going to answer our prayers. Generally speaking, we believe God is able to answer our prayers. But that may not be enough. The real question is, do we believe God is willing? When we understand that God is willing to answer our prayers, it makes it much easier for us to wait for His answer.

When we trust, we're making an investment. Typically we expect to reap a return on our investments within a certain time frame. But with real trust, we put confidence in something without knowing when we'll get a return, yet we refuse to stop believing that what we hope for will come to pass.

You never want to put this much trust in mankind. The Bible says, "It is better to trust in the LORD than to put confidence in man" (Ps. 118:8). And again, "Do not put your trust in princes, nor in a son of man, in whom there is no help" (Ps. 146:3).

It's sad to say, but it's true. Most human beings will take, take, take, and never give. When it comes to us trusting God, we need to realize that He may not send the return right away. But I want you to trust God so much in this season that you know He is going to bring the answer after a while. The Bible says that God is faithful to complete the work He has begun in us (Phil. 1:6). We will see a return if we do not lose heart (Gal. 6:9). Trusting in God is not like trusting in a trade market, where we expect a return immediately. His return comes according to His time clock, in His perfect timing, in due season. We can be confident of that.

Waiting and trusting God is all about knowing that His timing is always perfect. So even though we want Him to bless us right now, we don't stop trusting that He's going to bless us eventually. One of the greatest tests of our faith and trust in the Lord is that we still believe in Him even when He doesn't move when we want Him to move.

This is something we need to grasp: waiting is a part of receiving. If we receive everything we want exactly at the time we want it, we will never truly understand what it means to trust. I declare to you right now that you will receive the thing you're waiting for in God's perfect timing. He will distribute to you the very thing that you have prayed for.

You have to be excited about this. Even though you're

still waiting for the answer, the answer will come. Let me encourage you to make a faith exchange. Your faith will begin to work as you trust God. As your faith works, the exchange is being prepared. God is working on the answer. Understand that you will not receive what you're trusting God for when you want to receive it, but it will come at the perfect moment.

Before I go any further, I want to be clear about something: you will not receive what you're seeking simply because you want it. We will discuss this more in later chapters, but let me say now that the answer you can get excited about receiving from the Lord is the one that is in line with God's will for your life and His Word. How can we know that our desires are in line with God's will for us? The Bible says that we should delight ourselves in the Lord, and He will give us the desires of our hearts (Ps. 37:4). This verse lets me know that when we delight in God, our hearts' desires will line up with His.

When what you're seeking is in agreement with God's will for you, you can know without a doubt that even if you have to wait for a while, God is working on your behalf. Even if you can't tell what He's doing, He is working to bring the answer to your prayers.

As you wait, trust God. When you trust God, you have no room for doubt. When you trust God, you have no room for worry. Your exchange will come.

The person who trusts God at the highest level never doubts what God can and will do. The Word declares in James 1:6 that we should "ask in faith, without wavering. For he who wavers is like a wave of the sea, driven and tossed with the wind." That word *waver* means to doubt.

Don't doubt. When God makes a promise, you have to trust Him enough to know that if He said it, it will be done. So stop doubting and expecting an immediate exchange on your faith. God is going to move on your behalf, but it's going to take your being patient enough to wait on Him. If you try to make something happen yourself, it is going to fail. God never fails.

DON'T TRUST THE POWERLESS!

How often do we forget that God is all-powerful, then put our trust in so many other things, expecting them to give us the answers we need? How many times have we trusted in a source that was naturally powerful and forgot all about the fact that our supernatural source is all-powerful? For some reason it is hard to understand why that happens. The truth of the matter is, we trust in ourselves more than we trust God! This has to stop! God created us. God knows all, sees all, and is everywhere at the same time. We know this. We rejoice about this. We give Him praise every single day for being all-powerful. We call Him God Almighty, which means that God's power is limitless. So, for us to know this and still not put our total trust in Him demonstrates that we have a problem.

How do we refuse to trust in a power-filled God? I get excited about the fact that God can do anything, so I choose to trust Him. Our God cannot fail. We believe this to be a fact. We worship God based on His perfection, knowing that the answers to all our needs and desires are wrapped up in Him. I want to encourage you to trust in the One who knows it all. Trust in the One who holds all power in His hands. Trust in the One who cannot ever be a failure. Our God makes no mistakes.

It's a sad phenomenon when we go through life and end up regretting that, with the almighty, all-powerful God right in front of us, we neglected to trust Him. Why put your energy or your faith into things that will fail? There have been so many times in my life when I knew that something had the potential to fail, and I still trusted in that thing. I wish, on so many occasions, I would have put my trust in God instead. It's like the old saying: when you know better, do better. As soon as I began to recognize that one of the greatest benefits of being a child of God is being able to receive clear guidance from Him, I realized I didn't have to struggle and I didn't have to suffer in my waiting. I can trust in the all-knowing, all-powerful God. That He has all power in His hands is reason enough for us to relinquish our trust in other things and submit our trust to Him. I want to encourage you at this very moment: don't trust in the powerless.

A powerless source can do nothing for you. A powerless source cannot heal you. A powerless source cannot bring increase to you. A powerless source cannot renew your strength during this season of waiting. Waiting is not easy, but I can testify that waiting is easier when you are trusting in the right source. Knowing who God is makes waiting easy. God has you. The almighty One, who is all-powerful, is in control of your life, so let Him do the work. In fact, let me take that a step further: let God complete the work.

Too often, perhaps without realizing it, we think we have more power than God. We think we have the knowledge and ability to complete the work we need done in our lives, but eventually we find out that our brains can't even understand the capacity at which we would need to operate to finish the work ourselves. Here's some bad news, though it's good news at the same time: we are powerless. We have only an element of power because the powerful One lives inside of us. We do not carry the power in our own wills. We don't have the power in our own abilities. All of the power belongs to God.

I want to challenge you to make a commitment right now. Do as the Bible says in Psalm 37:5: "Commit your way to the LORD; trust also in Him, and He will bring it to pass." Make a declaration to yourself that this will be the last moment that you try to fix or even change your situation on your own. Make a commitment to yourself that you will submit to the power of God and no longer submit to the power of you. Your power may last for a short while, but it will not last forever. Commit yourself to submit your trust to the One whose power is everlasting.

As the Bible declares, from everlasting to everlasting, God will be God (Ps. 90:2). He knows the end from the beginning (Isa. 46:10). He knows our thoughts and our feelings. God knows it all. God sees it all. And God is all-powerful. So don't put your trust in the powerless; put your trust in the powerful. This is the only way any of us will get satisfying results.

If you want to continue to live your life being heartbroken or dissatisfied with the results you gain, keep trusting in the limited power sources made available to you. If you want to keep being lost, trying to find your way or wondering when things will get better, keep trusting in powerless sources. But if you're the type of person who says, "I believe that God is going to get me through this, and when I come out, I'm coming out stronger; I'm coming out better; I'm coming out wiser," then take a big leap of faith and trust in the Lord! He is all-powerful. Trust in God Almighty, the One whose power is limitless!

PRAY!

Father God, I pray that from this moment forward I will faithfully trust You even when I don't understand Your plans. I will not trust in my own ways, for You are my source of strength. I thank You for guiding me every day, in Jesus's name, amen.

NOW, DECLARE!

- I will trust in the Lord every day of my life (Prov. 3:5).

- I will not lean on my own understanding or my own interpretation of my journey (Prov. 3:5–6).

- My life is on the right track because I trust God's plan (Prov. 3:6).

- I am not afraid to step out on faith based on God's instructions (Josh. 1:9).

- I will see the goodness of God in the land of the living (Ps. 27:13).

Chapter 2

IT'S ALL ABOUT SEEING
WHAT GOD SEES

My GRANDFATHER OFTEN tells his congregation a story about something that took place many years ago when he pastored a very small church in Newburgh, New York. I love hearing the story because it involves me. I've always loved church. Moreover, I've always loved seeing churches grow. One day when I was about seven years old, my grandfather and I were sitting at home talking. All of a sudden he said, "Let's go down to the church." I quickly got dressed, because I loved to go to the church with my papa. He took me into the empty sanctuary, stood me in the back, and said, "Close your eyes." So with a great big smile on my face, I closed my eyes.

Wondering what my grandfather was up to, I quickly opened one eye and closed it just as quickly when I saw him looking at me. He said, "Marcus, imagine the church being full of people." I waited about ten seconds, and he then asked me, "What do you see?" I said, "Papa, I don't see anything." He began to laugh hysterically, hoping that my answer would have been that I saw the church full. But being seven years old, I only knew to say exactly what my eyes let me see, which was darkness.

What I found out later in life was that my grandfather wanted me to use my imagination and see the church full of people. He saw it, and that vision actually came to pass. That's the same way God invites us to see the invisible. He will allow us to be in a place that needs to be developed, and He will challenge our faith by pushing us to see what we don't see.

Our waiting season is like this as well. God will put us in a position and tell us to close our eyes and see into the future. It is as 1 Samuel 12:16 says, "Even now, take your stand and see this great thing which the LORD is doing before your eyes." I believe even now, as you are waiting for your miracle, as you are waiting for things to get better for you, God has stood you up in the middle of your empty situation and is asking you, "What do you see?" Many of us are like my seven-year-old self. We don't see anything. We see only what is physically there. But through experiences like the one I had with my grandfather, I've learned how to rejoice that what I see now will not be what I see forever. If my grandfather invited me back to that same spot in an empty church and asked me the same question, my answer would be different now.

I don't want you to agree with the enemy and only see the worst for your life. I don't want you to be down and miss out on seeing the good. Even in your waiting season, what do you see? Do you see yourself stuck in the same negative place forever? Or do you see yourself breaking through the worst season of your life? I want you to smile because you can see your reason to smile. I want you to see yourself better than the way everyone else sees you.

My papa would always tell me, "You have to see it before you see it, or you never will see it." In other words, if you don't see beyond your natural circumstances now, you'll never be able to see your future. If you see yourself broke, you'll stay broke. If you see yourself sick, you'll stay sick. If you see yourself lonely, you'll always feel lonely. Understand this: If you see yourself healed, healing will come. If you see yourself wealthy, wealth will come. If you see yourself married, marriage will come. Your future will be produced based on the seeds you sow now.

What type of seeds are you sowing? If you decide to sow the seeds of greatness, a harvest of greatness will come forth. Don't allow yourself to sow seeds of negativity. If you see the bad only, the bad will continue to produce itself in your life. But if you decide to see the good while the bad is in front of you, knowing that the good is on its way, the good will take over the bad.

The enemy is the one who shows you the negative stuff. The devil and his demons want you to see only your problems. God wants you to see your promise. God wants you to see that things will get better for you if you just believe. Satan wants you to believe that trouble will last forever. God wants you to see that trouble doesn't last always. That is certainly a reason to rejoice while you're in your waiting season. Because you can see beyond this season, start rejoicing for what you see in the future.

I heard a great prophet of God speak these words: "I see

you in the future, and you look much better than you look right now." Don't make decisions based upon what you see through your natural eyes. Learn how to see through the eyes of God. We already know that God is perfect in all His ways. So God is certainly going to show you what His will is for your life. And when God allows you to see your thing, He's showing you flawless things. There is no limit to what God can do. There are no flaws in what God shows you. What do you see?

I challenge you to take a break from this book, even now. Close your eyes and just picture your future. I know for a fact that what you see is better than where you are right now.

SIGHT

The Bible says, "We walk by faith, not by sight" (2 Cor. 5:7). This is one of the most encouraging scriptures in the Bible for many reasons. For me, this scripture helps me to understand how to gain strength during my waiting time. The word *walk* used in this verse refers to how we live. So it's safe to even declare that we *live* by faith and not by sight. This scripture encourages us not to live by what we see in the natural but to live by faith.

There are so many people in the world, believers and nonbelievers, who live by what they see with their natural eyes. But as believers, you and I must go above and beyond and not live by our natural eyesight. We must live by our supernatural eyesight. This is called living by faith.

Natural sight is not a terrible thing. It gives you the ability to engage and be aware of the natural world around you. Visual perception is a gift from God for our natural use. We are able to take in concrete or fixed images and draw conclusions about circumstances or environments. But without spiritual sight working along with our natural sight, we only get a glimpse of our future—a momentary or partial view of the possibilities of life. This is why we cannot live by natural sight alone. We need the full picture.

If you live by sight, you live with a limited view of what God has in store for you. Even though natural eyesight helps to make you aware of some good things in your life, it still doesn't warrant your living solely on its ability. Natural eyesight only confirms your current situation and reality. And with that, what you see in the natural can be very discouraging. You may be hoping for a mate, but your natural sight shows you that you're single. Your natural sight shows you all your friends and coworkers who are in happy romantic relationships. With your natural sight, you can't see yourself as happily married sometime soon. All you can see with your natural eyes is your singleness.

You may be believing God for a better job or your own business, but your natural eyes only allow you to see the job that you currently show up to every day. Your natural eyes show you that you don't have the credentials, connections, or money to move up or start your own business. Your natural eyes show you the wealth and prosperity of others while you see the low or negative balance in your bank account.

Your natural eyes will allow you to see that doctor's bad report. Your natural eyes will allow you to see yourself as sick with no chance of being healed.

Do you understand what I'm trying to tell you? Even

17

though our natural eyesight is real, we need to activate our spiritual sight—the eyes of faith—to clearly see the promise and future God has for us. We need to hear and obey the Word of God and refuse to walk or live solely by sight. The Bible says in Mark 11:24, "Therefore I say to you, whatever things you ask when you pray, believe that you will receive them, and you will have them." Pray and believe God for the blessings of your future. Pray about what you want to see. You will be stuck in the same place forever if you live by your natural eyesight.

I remember, when I first began in ministry, how it was a struggle to set up all those chairs week after week and never see them filled. It was hard for my ministry team and me to see how many people were not coming to the church. I remember one Sunday a powerful woman of God came to a service. I guess she could see the disappointed look on my face at the attendance. She came to me after the service and said, "Pastor Marcus, what you see now is not really what you see."

I didn't understand what she meant at the time, but I recognized the revelation behind her words later. She was basically telling me that what I see through my natural eyes is not my final stop. I want to encourage you at this moment. If you are in a place that looks horrible or a season where everything around you looks as if it can never grow and produce, know this: what you see is not really what you see. Your natural eyesight is just for you to see in the natural. But God has given us sight beyond the natural. The devil and his demons wish for you to keep your natural eyes open so you can only see where you are right now. But you are going to grow beyond this.

You've been waiting for God to change things for you, and it looks as if it's taking forever. Remember what I said: what you see is not your reality.

I want to challenge you to see beyond the natural. See beyond this temporary view. This is just a glimpse of your life. What God has for you is so much greater than what you see right now. Try this every morning when you wake up. Get out of the bed, go to your nearest mirror, look at yourself, and say these words aloud: "I see myself

> You will be stuck in the same place forever if you live by your natural eyesight.

better than this." Take some time while you pray and lay your hands over your natural eyes and declare, "I walk by faith and not by sight." Anoint your eyes so that you will begin to see beyond your natural circumstances. Continue to believe God that what you see now with your natural sight is not going to be what you see forever.

VISION

Sight has its value in the natural, but vision has much more value when we talk about supernatural power. Sight can only show you the present. Vision shows you the future. God gave me this definition of vision: vision is your supernatural imagination that you expect to become your reality. So when you imagine something that's not in front of you, your vision is being activated. I'll take it a step further and say true vision is our supernatural imagination inspired by God.

It's one thing to have a good imagination, but it's a greater thing to have a God imagination. You could come up with some good ideas in life, but when you come up with a God idea, it's an idea you can't even understand yourself without the help of the Lord.

Do you have vision? Without a vision for your future, you really have nothing to look forward to. A person with no vision only looks forward to being in the same place they are in right now. A person with no vision doesn't have anything to look forward to other than a repeat of their current situation.

Don't put yourself in position to just keep repeating the same cycle of life. While you are waiting on God, your vision should cause you to rejoice with expectation for what is to come.

Watching your vision before it comes to pass is like watching your future as a movie. You might not be there right now, but when your vision is activated, you are there in a supernatural realm.

When you have vision, you are able to see your future while you are in the middle of your current situation. With vision you're able to observe things that you cannot see in the natural. When you have the right vision for your life, it will increase commitment and energize you. Vision helps you to establish a standard of excellence in your life. Vision is how you connect your present and your future. While you're in your waiting season, understand this: if you have no vision, there will be no change.

Here are four keys to keeping your vision alive.

1. Create a vision statement.

Put together a vision statement while you are preparing for this next phase of your life. Make sure that your vision statement inspires you and gives meaning to your life and your endeavors. You could be chasing your dreams for a very long time and fighting for change, but if you don't see the end result before you get there, you will be chasing your dreams and fighting the fight of your life forever. Prepare yourself for the results now.

2. Connect with other visionaries.

Make sure you're connected to people who have a vision for their lives as well. If you stay connected to people who have no vision for their own lives, they will end up being vision blockers in your life.

3. Conduct periodic self-inventories.

It's very important for you to do a self-inventory while you are on this journey. There may be some things that you need to get rid of so you can see your vision more clearly. Your attitude has to be in the right place. Your level of commitment and dedication to your vision must be at the right level. You must be connected to the right people who will help you along the way.

4. Act on it.

When you have a vision for your life, it gives meaning to your waiting season. Don't just have a vision and not act on it. The Bible tells us that as the body without a spirit is dead, so is faith without works (James 2:26). When you act on your vision, it gives your vision advance purpose. The Bible also tells us, "Where there is no vision, the people perish" (Prov. 29:18). This scripture doesn't describe physical death but spiritual death. So many people go through life dying a spiritual death because they have no vision.

They have nothing to look forward to. They have nothing to work toward. Do not die while you're waiting for God to fix your situation. You can live through this waiting season by working your vision.

There are so many definitions of the word *success*. I believe that success doesn't happen when we finish our vision but while we are working toward the completion of our vision. Right now you may be saying, "Pastor Marcus, I've been waiting forever, but I'm working my vision." That's good news! While you are working your vision, you're already successful.

Your vision gives your work meaning. It helps you to establish a high standard of excellence, perfection, joy, and integrity. Your vision for the future should motivate you to keep on pressing and not give up. When my grandfather stood me up in the back of the empty church, told me to close my eyes, and asked me what I saw, vision would have shown me that the church was full and not empty.

Make sure that your supernatural imagination overrides your natural eyesight. Don't get stuck seeing temporary things. See supernatural things.

Having an awesome vision for your life is the first step in your planning for the future. Get your vision together. Get a set of ideas and priorities that help you picture the future. Discover the qualities that make you special and unique. Even though your vision can change over time, your vision is always attainable. It engages your heart and your spirit. Your vision will help lead you to your goal. Vision makes your waiting experience worthwhile. Let your supernatural imagination increase your expectation for what can soon be your reality. Let your supernatural imagination be the fuel to the vehicle you use throughout your life journey. I declare right now that your vision shall come to pass!

FOCUS

One of the hardest things for me to do in school when I was growing up was to stay focused. OK, I admit it. I probably wasn't the best student because I got bored so fast, but I guess I turned out OK. Focus is about being properly engaged. When you're focused, it means you're interested. A person who is focused is paying particular attention to someone or something. A person who is focused is not easily distracted.

The best time for the devil and his demons to distract you is when you're on the right track but you're having a rough time. One of the best ways to know that you're on the right track is if things come to throw you off track. I often say this: the only reason you were attacked with distraction is because the enemy already knows you are effective. A person who isn't focused on anything that has to do with God doesn't get attacked by the enemy. Why? The enemy doesn't have to distract someone who is already distracted. He already has the person on his side. There is no need for him to seek after that person hoping to devour him or her with distractions.

While you are waiting on God and seeing through His eyes, you have to stay focused. It's not until you start focusing on the good things that the devil and his demons will try to use anything and everything to get you off your course. You may be reading this right now, and while I am encouraging you with these words, a distraction may come. If you share the same testimony that I do, you would agree that it seems like every time you start getting closer and closer to your miracle, a distraction comes.

Distractions come in the form of problems. Just when it seems as if everything is fixed, here comes another broken situation thrown at you. The devil and his demons do this to make you feel as if you're always going to be faced with problems. But the devil is a liar! You will not lose track. You will not get off course. You will remain focused on what God has for you. And that's the bottom line.

You're not going to pay attention to the negative signs the enemy tries to show you. I want you to be determined. Do not listen to the negative voices inside your head. These voices come to get you off track. I want you to focus on your healing, if you are sick; your financial increase, if you need a financial miracle; your marriage, if it needs to be restored. You may be a pastor reading this right now, and you're focusing on the empty seats you see on Sundays. I want you to focus on the souls that can be saved and get excited about what God has shown you.

Let your vision be your cynosure. Let the blessings of your future be the center of your attention and admiration. A person who is dedicated to staying focused will stay focused and work hard. Make a note to yourself in this season of your life. Tell yourself, "Don't get thrown off by the foolish things in life." Dedicate yourself to staying positive. Even though things get hard during this season, you must stay ambitious. Set your goals and make your plans. Work hard and stick to your work. When you work hard and stick to your work, you will reach your goal. But you must stay focused.

Keep seeing through the eyes of God. Whenever God sets out to do something, it always gets done. We serve a focused God. He cannot fail or be distracted. This is why we rejoice over what the Scripture says: "For all the promises of God in Him are 'Yes,' and in Him 'Amen,' to the glory of God through us" (2 Cor. 1:20).

Stay focused even when things get hard. Breakthrough is sure to come, but it may take time, and it will require dedication, willpower, and sacrifice. When you're focused on the right things, you will have to push yourself to the max. Even though temptations arise, you have to refuse to yield to them. By the time you reach your goal, you will recognize that it was all worth it.

One of the most important pieces to getting your breakthrough is having the discipline to do what's right even when you don't feel like it. Stop getting distracted by things that have nothing to do with your future blessings. Keep your eyes on God. You cannot build a better life for yourself if you're not focused on the plan. Seeing through the eyes of God requires vision, work, and focus. Zoom in on the positive detail that God lays before you.

PLANNING

If I am on my way out of my house and someone tells me it's going to rain, the proper thing to do would be to dress for rainy weather and take my umbrella with me. Grabbing my umbrella, even though the rain isn't falling yet, is a sign that I am planning ahead for what is coming. If a person tells me it's going to rain and I purposely leave my umbrella at home, that's a sign that I don't believe, or care, what the individual has told me.

25

This is the same way many people do God. God warns us and makes promises to us. When God speaks to us and tells us about our future, He expects us to believe Him. He expects us as His children to believe the word that He speaks. The greatest act of faith for a believer is to plan according to what God says. If God speaks to you and you refuse to make plans based on what He said to you, that is the sign that you don't believe His word will come to pass. It's like slapping God in His face. That is certainly a dangerous idea, but it happens often.

God has made promises to you and me, and I believe He is waiting to see whether or not we believe Him. We prove that we really believe Him by planning accordingly. To make plans is to be detailed in your proposal for doing something. Planning reviews your intentions or your decision about what you are going to do. While you are in your waiting season, you need to make some decisions about your future. You need to plan for the blessing.

When God speaks to me and reveals things about my future, I start making arrangements in advance. I believe that when I make arrangements for my miracle in advance, I'm showing God that I trust Him.

Don't just wait for God to work a miracle in your life and not do anything. Start putting things in order. Start positioning yourself now for the miracle. Begin to organize your life as if the miracle has already arrived. Don't wait until the blessing comes to start adjusting to it. Act as though you have the blessing now. This is a part of our planning for the blessings of our future. When you plan based on the promises of God, God gets to see your intentions. He gets to see what you're truly aiming for.

I want to encourage you to begin your process of making decisions for your future in order to achieve your premeditated success. There are things you need to achieve now before your ultimate achievement. For the faith-filled believer, planning is not optional. Planning is a requirement. When you fail to plan, you plan to fail. Believe it or not, there are so many believers who are uncomfortable planning. Planning is a part of walking by faith and not by sight.

A very difficult element of planning is planning in the face of conflict. There are some things that will catch you by surprise while you're planning for your future, but they should not restrict you from determining your steps of achievement before you reach your goal. A great writer once said that "a goal without a plan is just a wish."[1] Don't spend your waiting season wishing for a miracle without planning for the miracle. As I once heard it said, plan your work and work your plan.

You must understand that success doesn't just happen. You have to plan for it. And then your plan is only as good as how it looks through the eyes of God. God's vision for your life leaves nothing to be desired. He sees your end and declares that it will be greater than your beginning. This is why you need to lean in to His plans for your life. As you begin to prepare for your future blessings, know that you don't have to come up with a plan by yourself. You can follow the flawless plan of God!

A person who has a vision for their great future is a person who knows the results of great planning. The earlier you start to plan and the earlier you involve God in your plans, the sooner you will be able to see the manifestations of your vision. But even if you are well into your journey, it's never too late to start planning, to write out your vision, and to make plans for your future. Regardless of where you are in life, understand that real planning will prepare you for real results.

There's something about planning that a lot of people don't like to think about, but it's true. Failure is a part of planning. Nobody likes to fail, and failure can sometimes cause people to stop planning for fear of failing again. When my plans fail, I just see it as a reason to make more plans. You only fail when you quit after the failure. You succeed after failure when you decide to come up with another plan. The best part about failing is that you get to find not just a new plan but a better plan. I once read, "If plan A doesn't work, the alphabet has 25 more letters."[2] In other words, one plan may fail, but don't let that be your reason for giving up. There are so many more things God can introduce to you in the meantime.

When you don't have a plan for your life, it's like being a ship in the middle of the sea without a sail. You have nothing to work toward. There's nothing pushing you to a destination. Poor planning will lead to poor results. Take time to prepare for the best. Seeing through the eyes of God will motivate you to plan for what's already done. Show God how much you believe what He said by making plans to be prepared for the promises yet to come.

TEMPORARY POSITION

One of my favorite songs in the world is a gospel song written by the late reverend Timothy Wright that talks about the joy that comes when we realize that trouble doesn't last forever. This song reminds me that the blessings are coming soon despite my present trouble. Maybe you're in the middle of a storm right now. The truth of the matter is, this storm called waiting isn't comfortable. It seems as if you have been waiting forever! This season can be one of the most frustrating times of your life, but because you know and trust God, you haven't quit.

The joy that you can gain while you're waiting, even though this waiting is frustrating, comes from knowing that your current situation is only temporary. This season is not your forever season. Things are going to get better soon. In the meantime, understand that this temporary position is preparing you for everlasting power. During this season you are perfectly positioned to build strength in areas in which you are weak. You have the opportunity not only to pray that God will help you go through the storm but also to ask God to help you grow through this storm, so when you get to that place of promise, you will have the character to sustain and maintain it.

There's so much we can learn while we are in these temporary positions. If God handed every miracle to us without our knowing how to endure a tough season, we would not be able to handle the miracle and enjoy it at the same time. God allows us to go through these temporary seasons of discomfort because He is preparing us for a long-lasting season of pleasure. This painful waiting season is only going to last for a limited time. It is not permanent.

Waiting time is provisional, an interim experience. I've found that in my life God has used the wait to transition me from one level of greatness to a higher level of greatness. So when I get ready to complain about why it's taking so long for God to move, I just remind myself, "The longer I wait, the greater the blessing."

Let God increase your strength during your waiting season. The Bible says that the hearts of those who wait on the Lord will be strengthened (Ps. 27:14). I've written this book to tell you to be of good courage while you wait for your future blessings, because they are coming. Just knowing that my blessings are on the way even if I don't see them with my natural eyes causes me to shout when I sing the song "Trouble Don't Last Always."

Get this in your heart right now: Sickness is temporary. Depression is temporary. Financial lack is temporary. Loneliness is temporary. The discord that may exist in your family or relationships is temporary. All of the pain you feel right now is not permanent. It only exists in the moment for a limited period of time.

Paul said in Romans 8:28 that all things are working for your good. If you decide to stop seeing through the eyes of God because of a temporary experience, you will miss out on everlasting victory. When God sees your problems, He sees a temporary situation. This is why it's important for you to practice seeing through God's eyes and not your own. The apostle Paul says it well:

> Our light affliction, which lasts but for a moment, works for us a far more exceeding and eternal weight of glory, while we do not look at the things which are seen, but at the things which are not seen. For the things which are seen are temporal, but the things which are not seen are eternal.
>
> —2 CORINTHIANS 4:17–18

Every time you're faced with a painful situation, use the power in your mouth to speak out loud and declare, "This will not last forever." There is so much comfort in knowing that every wrong thing that's happening in your life is temporary. Some people find themselves spending a lot of time focusing on temporary things, and then they wonder why things never change. The negative elements of your life are just temporary. If you focus on those negative elements, you'll miss out on the everlasting positive elements, the eternal elements.

> Your temporary position is preparing you for everlasting power.

Don't get attached to those temporary things. Just flow with it, knowing that a great change is coming. Your struggle is temporary, but your strength is forever. The place that God is taking you is not temporary. God doesn't work temporary miracles. He allows you to experience the valley for a limited time so that He can bring you out. God is a delivering God. You would never know His delivering power firsthand if He didn't allow you to go through some things sometimes. But I'm glad He has already overcome for us. We will be all right when we recognize that God is in control.

I remember when I was going through the toughest season of my life. It almost brings me to tears as I write about it now. I really thought that what I was going through was going to be my forever situation. If someone would have told me it was only temporary, I never would have had thoughts of suicide, which would have been my taking matters into my own hands to fix my own problem,

31

without actually fixing it. I would have allowed a temporary experience to cause me to miss out on everlasting joy. I'm so glad that God shook me, woke me up, and helped me to realize that my experience wouldn't be everlasting. God helped me recognize that the feeling of defeat was only a temporary condition.

You may find yourself temporarily losing hope or love, but the good thing about that feeling is this: God never temporarily loves you. He always loves you, and this is why He will give you an opportunity to recognize that your best is ahead. You may be carrying a temporary burden right now, but a permanent blessing has already been prepared for you. Your waiting season is a temporary position as you prepare for your eternal reward.

PRAY!

Dear Lord, I thank You for allowing me to see what You see. Help me to understand that my current circumstance will not be what I see forever. Help me, Lord, to never give up but to hang on until I see the full manifestation of my miracle. In Jesus's name, amen.

NOW, DECLARE!

- I declare that my eyes are open to see the goodness of the Lord (Ps. 27:13).

- I will not live based on what I see in the natural; I walk by faith and not by sight (2 Cor. 5:7).

- My eyes are blinded to fearful elements in my life (Ps. 23:4).

- I am not overwhelmed by the burdens of the enemy; no weapon formed against me will prosper (Isa. 54:17).

- I am blessed because I choose to obey God's Word (Luke 11:28).

Chapter 3

IT'S ALL ABOUT HOW
YOU WAIT AND PRAY

I T IS TRUE that prayer changes things. Our decision to
pray is one of the greatest signs of our faith. There's certainly power in prayer. When we or a family member
or friend are sick and we don't know what to do, we do
know to pray. When there is a financial storm in our lives
and we don't understand how God will take care of the
situation, we know to pray. When we watch the news and
hear of all the tragedies that take place in our world, we
know to pray.

We know that there is power in prayer. When we give
our problems over to God in prayer, He will move on
our behalf. There have been many times in my life when
I was struggling with an issue, and after I prayed, God
responded quickly to meet the need. Prayer was the only
thing that brought breakthrough. The Bible tells us to be
anxious for nothing but in everything by prayer and supplication to make our requests known unto God (Phil.

4:6). Prayer is one of the greatest acts of faith that we could practice.

The Bible tells us in Luke 18:1 that we ought to always pray, and in 1 Thessalonians 5:17 we're commanded to pray without ceasing. God has commanded us to pray because He knows how much prayer benefits us, especially during a season of waiting. Through prayer we not only talk to God, but we also are able to hear the Lord speak to us. We receive instructions, encouragement, and strength, and more valuable than anything else, we invoke God's presence. With God's presence comes His peace, as well as His power and authority to intervene on our behalf.

Consider this: if someone is sick or in pain, that person can pick up the phone and dial 911, and a rescue unit will respond. But if that person refuses to call for emergency help and continues to sit in sickness and pain, one can assume that individual doesn't realize he has the power to call for help. There are a lot of people who treat God the same way. They have a need, and their patience to wait for the answer is running dry. God has made Himself available to help. His Word says that He is "a very present help" in times of trouble (Ps. 46:1, KJV). All they have to do is pray in faith, and God will respond (Matt. 21:22; Mark 11:24). But many, perhaps overcome by fear or discouragement, or because they have a habit of expecting the worst, don't call on Him.

Listen, God will never overlook or ignore your prayers. He says, "Call to Me, and I will answer you, and show you great and mighty things which you do not know" (Jer. 33:3). He desires to show you the things He has promised for you on the other side of your wait.

As I said before, it's not always easy to wait. But prayer helps us humble ourselves and submit our spirits to the timing of the Lord. They used to say in the old church, God may not answer your prayers when you want Him to, but He will answer right on time! This statement is such an encouragement to me. During our waiting season we need to know that God has already set His promises for us in motion. Prayer helps us wait patiently on the Lord.

THE RIGHT WAY TO PRAY

We want to do things right. I've never met a person who enjoys making mistakes. We go to school as children, and some of us go to the next level and finish college, all for the purpose of learning more so we can do things the right way. I believe that you're the type of person who desires to do things to the best of your ability. That goes for your relationships, your business or career, and most importantly your relationship with God.

I always say the best gift to mankind is the opportunity to have a real relationship with God. My heart's desire is to make sure that my relationship with God is strong. In all I do, I want God to be pleased with me. I trust that is your heart's desire as well. So let's make sure that we pray the right way.

Growing up in church, I've heard a lot of different prayer styles. Some were unorthodox, and some were effective. In your waiting season you could be experiencing a delay in receiving a blessing because you are not praying effectively. I'll take time to expound on this more as we journey through this chapter. For now I want to share eight ways to pray that I've found to be a blessing during a season of waiting.

1. Pray aloud.

Prayer is a way for us to humbly communicate praise and worship to God, and to seek His face with all sincerity. Because God loves us, He will respond when we cry out to Him, but I have found that we must call out to Him. For me, this means I have to pray aloud. God knows our thoughts and hears us whether we pray out loud or silently. But praying aloud helps me focus my attention on bringing my requests to God, and when I do, a sense of expectation begins to rise up in my heart. When I speak my request out loud, my need is no longer just in my heart or in my thoughts. I'm bringing it out in the open before an almighty God who cares about what concerns me and will respond to my prayers.

You may say, "I can't pray aloud at work or when I'm in public places." If that's the case, then whisper. In whatever way you need, be intentional about taking your requests to God. Don't let the fact that you're not at home in your prayer closet keep you from praying.

Also, don't wait until you're in a crisis to go before God in prayer. Make prayer a daily habit. When you get up in the morning or when you have some time alone during the day, purposefully spend time with God. If you make time in your schedule to seek God, you will be able to pray, praise, and worship out loud without worrying about being judged or disturbing other people.

2. Pray effectual prayers.

James 5:16 tells us the effectual, fervent prayer of the righteous avails much. When your prayers are effectual, they are effective. They accomplish their mission. It is God's job to answer the prayer; it is our job to trust that He is able and willing to answer it. You need to have a strong belief that God is all-powerful and what you are praying for surely will come to pass.

James 5:16 also says to pray fervently. When your prayers are fervent, it means they are passionate. You should pray with intensity. You should pray with extreme force and strength. When you go to the Lord with effectual, fervent prayer, your prayers are serious.

When I was a child, my grandfather would tell me that I should pray earnestly. I would ask, "Why should I pray honestly?" And then I learned that the word wasn't *honestly*; it was *earnestly*. Our prayers should always be backed by sincere and intense conviction that all the promises of God are yes in Him and amen, and that God will answer our prayers in His timing and in His way.

It's easy to pray fervently when we are passionately concerned about what we are praying for. The dictionary defines *fervent* as "marked by great intensity of feeling."[1] I've also heard some people use *fervent* to mean violent or furious. When we pray, we cause damage to the enemy. We pray with extreme force. But when we pray, we are not angry. We are praying with power and authority, doing damage to the devil's plan for our lives. As we pray, God is destroying what the enemy intended to destroy us.

3. Pray with understanding.

Praying with understanding is about praying with the realization that prayer is for our benefit and not God's benefit. We need God. We need His power. Hebrews 4:16 tells us to come with confidence to the throne of grace that we may obtain mercy and find grace to help in time of need. We need God, and when we understand that God wants to meet our needs, we will pray with confidence, knowing that He will answer.

4. Pray with joy.

We must pray with joy, believing that God is going to bless us with our hearts' desire. The apostle Paul said in Philippians 1:4, "In every prayer of mine for you all, I have always made requests with joy." Paul was joyful and thankful as he prayed.

5. Pray from a place of righteousness.

God hears the prayers of the righteous. I believe that when we live right, it places us in the perfect position to receive God's best. Psalm 34:17 says, "The righteous cry out, and the LORD hears, and delivers them out of all their troubles." This verse lets us know that the ears of the Lord are open to the righteous. When we turn from our ungodly ways, He responds to our cry and delivers us from our troubles, seen and unseen.

6. Pray with humility.

I believe that God hears the prayers of the humble. When you humble yourself before God and live a God-fearing life, I believe that sets you up for God to hear and answer your prayers. Stay humble before the Lord. God will certainly extend His mercy to you. The Bible says, "God resists the proud, but gives grace to the humble" (James 4:6).

7. Pray with a sincere heart.

God wants to hear sincerity in our prayers. As you pray, be determined not to pray in vain. Hebrews 10:22 says, "Let us draw near with a true heart in full assurance of faith, having our hearts sprinkled to cleanse them from an evil conscience, and our bodies washed with pure water." The word translated "assurance" in this verse also means to be sincere. So pray genuinely.

8. Pray with a pure heart.

Make sure that your heart is in the right place. While you're waiting on God to release His blessings to you, your heart must be pure before Him. So next time you go to God in prayer, do some self-examination first. The Bible asks in Psalm 24, "Who may ascend the hill of the LORD? Who may stand in His holy place? He who has clean hands and a pure heart" (vv. 3–4). We draw near to the Lord when we pray. I see a pure heart as our access pass into the presence of the Lord.

The fact that you are still waiting on God to bless you and you are praying for God to move is a sign that you still have a chance to grow and get right with Him. The best thing you could do as it concerns your prayer life during this waiting season is to make sure you are praying the right way, allowing His will and presence to cause your heart's desires to line up with His will for your life.

Waiting and Praying Can Get Lonely

The waiting season can be very lonely—not just for those who are single when it comes to their romantic relationship status, but even for those who are married or have children. When you are waiting on God to work a miracle on your behalf, you can feel lonely. But you're not alone. God made Joshua a promise in the Bible, saying, "I will never leave you nor forsake you." (See Deuteronomy 31:6.) God makes this same promise to you today. Even though you feel as if you're alone in this season, I want you to agree with the promise of God.

David said in Psalm 23:4, "Even though I walk through the valley of the shadow of death, I will fear no evil; for You are with me." I want you to agree with God today. He is holding you by the hand even while you're waiting. God will not leave you alone while you wait. God stands with you while you wait. What a great joy to not have to be separated from Him during this season of your life. To know that God desires to be with us is a miracle in itself.

When you decide to fully come into agreement with God, you decide to become unified with Him. And wherever you go, God goes. Make a decision right now that even though you're waiting and wondering when God is going to move, you're going to be one with Him because you're going to agree with Him.

Obey the Lord. Don't allow negative thoughts to cause you to pull away from God. During the worst seasons of your life you should draw closer to God. The best relationship you and I could ever have is a true relationship with God.

PRAYING FOR ESCAPE

The waiting season can sometimes be troublesome and challenging, causing us to really press in to God for strength, safety, deliverance, and encouragement. But sometimes we face stormy seasons that are so trying, we just want out! Though there are times when we pray that God would bring us out of our troubles, I'd rather only pray those kinds of prayers when I'm in a time of trouble that I didn't get myself into.

In the Bible we read about how Daniel was thrown into the lions' den. Was that his fault? No. He was there because the people around him could not accept the fact that he wanted to worship the true and living God. To punish him, they decided to get the king to pass a law forbidding prayer to anyone but him. Those who violated the edict would be thrown into the lions' den. While this was a tough predicament, Daniel didn't necessarily bring that problem upon himself. We read in the Bible also about Shadrach, Meshach, and Abednego. They too had to endure a certain level of punishment because they chose to follow God's perfect will.

These are two examples of how you can end up in

> The best relationship you and I could ever have is a true relationship with God.

situations that aren't your fault because you chose not to step out of God's perfect will. These examples show that you may have to temporarily go through hardship as a result of obeying God's perfect will. Praying for a way out of a bad situation is certainly understandable. But these men couldn't circumvent the waiting season. While Daniel was in the lions' den, and while Shadrach, Meshach, and Abednego had to endure the fiery furnace, they were waiting for God to move.

These men prayed for escape after doing what God told them to do, but that is not always the way it goes with us. We don't always find ourselves praying prayers of escape because we were doing what God told us to do while waiting. If you're like me, you have found yourself asking God to rescue you from self-created messes. If that happens to you, don't feel as if life is over. The fact that you can still pray and ask God to pull you out is evidence that He still loves you and has something greater in store for you.

As I was sharing with you previously, at one time in my life I found myself in a terrible situation. I made a decision that I knew was not God's perfect will for my life, and I ended up having to survive in His permissive will for a season. Oftentimes, when I share my testimony, people ask me how I came out of that season. I always answer boldly, "I prayed, and God created a way of escape."

When I tell that testimony, looking back on my situation, it sounds easy, but it's not as easy as it seems. I mentioned Daniel in the lions' den and the three Hebrew boys in the fiery furnace to paint a picture for you. But you know as well as I do that some of your storms were not caused by others. Some of your storms, even the storm you may be in now, were caused by you. Our disobedience to God forces us into self-made fiery furnaces.

If you're in the lions' den of your life because you put yourself there, you need to pray for a way of escape so you can get out of God's permissive will and enter His perfect will. We will talk more completely about God's will in the next chapter, but I want you to see this now as it relates to how you should pray during your season of waiting if you find yourself in a lions' den.

You are in this less-than-ideal place because you were impatient, desperate, or tired. I've come to encourage you not to give up. Don't give in to making wrong decisions and doing your own thing. You don't want to be forced to pray for a way of escape. While you're waiting on God to do a new thing in your life, you shouldn't have to be stressed out, asking God to rescue you. Don't let bad choices land you in a place of confinement. This waiting season should be preparing you for your future blessings. You shouldn't be spending this time working to get away from self-created problems.

It is a blessing that God loves us so much that He hears the cries of His children and will rescue us from all our troubles. But we could better use our prayer time focusing on the next season of blessing rather than pleading for a way of escape from problems we created for ourselves.

In your waiting season, don't commit yourself to doing your will and make a habit of trusting that God will pull you out of your own mistakes. Paul asked in Romans 6:1, "Shall we continue in sin, that grace may abound?" (KJV). No! Don't take advantage of the power of God and repeatedly seek Him to pull you out of the lions' den or the fiery furnace that you created yourself. Disobedience is a dangerous thing. God will open doors of escape for you to help you get back in line with Him. But it is obedience to God that opens the door for you to be blessed.

45

Don't Command God

God is all-powerful. He is our Creator and our Shepherd. He's the ruler of heaven and earth. God is in charge, and even though He gave us dominion on earth, we have no right to command Him. However, some of us make the mistake of praying and making demands of God as if He were a genie in a bottle. Please be very careful how you approach God in prayer. Job learned this the hard way. After losing his children and his livelihood, Job cried out to God, accusing Him of treating him unfairly and asking God to explain Himself. God responded to him in chapters 38 to 42 of the Book of Job. He began by saying, "Who is this who darkens counsel by words without knowledge?" (Job 38:2). God went on to ask Job where he was when the foundations of the earth were laid, if he knew where the storehouses of snow were kept, or if he watched as the doe gave birth to her fawn.

Of course Job didn't know those things. He wasn't God—and that was God's point. When the Almighty explained why He was God and Job was not, all Job could do was repent: "Behold, I am vile; what shall I answer You? I will lay my hand over my mouth" (Job 40:4). I wish Job's story was enough to keep people from second-guessing God, but most of us have questioned Him at one time or another.

When I was in my early days of ministry, my grandfather taught me never to tell God what to do. What I should do is ask God for what I would like Him to do. It's just that simple. A wrong way to pray is praying as if you are God's boss. It sounds absurd, but do our prayers reflect the right understanding of who God is?

God is flawless, perfect in all His ways. He is our Father and master. When we pray, we need to pray to God with all due respect. Even though God is merciful and kind, we must remember that we are praying to the One who represents all authority.

Do you make demands of your boss or command him or her to do as you say? Most likely you listen to those in authority over you and try to carry out the instructions you are given. You interact with a level of trust that your boss is going to do the best that he or she can. If we can do this with humans, how much more should we be doing this with the Creator of the universe?

When you approach God making demands and showing disrespect, you will find yourself waiting forever for a miracle. One of the best ways to delay your blessing is to treat God as if He is unworthy of your consideration or respect. God is holy. He is worthy of praise and respect. Don't ever get to the point in your waiting season where you get so frustrated that you lose respect for God. Don't ever lose your deep admiration for God and His abilities, qualities, and what He's already done in your life.

Approaching God in reverence and humility demonstrate your understanding of who He is and the power He possesses. Remember this: God resists the proud but gives grace to the humble (Prov. 3:34). Only a proud man or woman would come to God without regard. In fact, when we pray, most times we kneel or bow to physically display our lowly state compared to the greatness of God. Of course, you can pray standing up or while driving, but kneeling and bowing are signs of humility and respect.

I respect God enough to come to Him as humbly as I

know how, first thanking Him for what He's done, asking for forgiveness of my sins, and then politely making my request known to Him. Humbly going to God with our questions, problems, and needs puts us in our rightful position as created beings in the presence of our Creator. As we respectfully inquire about our needs, we are to humbly wait for an answer from almighty God.

In Matthew 7:7 Jesus said that we should ask, seek, and knock. These three forms of prayer or requests come from positions of humility. When you demand that God do certain things, you're telling God that you have a right to make Him do what you want Him to do. When you make demands, you put yourself in a position of authority and attempt to overrule God. You are operating in pride, and as James 4:6 says, God resists the proud but gives grace to the humble.

Simply put, we can't give God orders. We are not God's management team. He doesn't need our counseling or our guidance. We are His children. We are His creation. God cannot benefit from our input. He operates perfectly without our hands being involved in His operations. He graciously allows us to cooperate with Him. He guides and counsels us. God manages our lives. And when we pray, we are humbly asking Him to help us understand what He allows so we can be in the perfect position to serve and please Him.

PRAY!

Father, I thank You for giving me the patience to wait. Help me to pray the right way as I wait on You. Thank You, Lord, for hearing my prayers and teaching me how to live in obedience to Your Word. Continue to shape me for this season of my life, in Jesus's name, amen.

NOW, DECLARE!

- I will worship while I wait for my prayers to be answered (1 Chron. 16:25).

- God hears my prayers, and He answers (Jer. 33:3).

- I declare that my waiting is renewing my strength (Isa. 40:31).

- I will not give up while I wait (2 Chron. 15:7).

- I will wait, worship, and win (Gal. 6:9).

Chapter 4

IT'S ALL ABOUT DISCERNING
GOD'S PERFECT WILL

MOST PEOPLE WRESTLE with knowing God's will for their lives. Maybe you are one of them. Since you're reading this book, I would guess you're the type of person who doesn't want anything more than to follow God and His plan for your life. Maybe you've been walking with God for some time, but you're not always certain you know what His will is for your life. So maybe from time to time you wonder, "What is God's will concerning me?"

As a pastor, the most common question people ask me is, "How do I figure out what God's will is for my life?" This is a very good question. As I said already, it's a great thing to even want to know what God desires for you. There are so many people in the world who attend church regularly but couldn't care less what God's will is for them. They want the benefits of knowing God without having a real relationship with Him.

Those who want to know the will of God for their life have a desire to please God. Why would anyone want to know God's will for his life if he had no intention of fulfilling His plan? It is a noble ambition to want to know God's will for you. God's will is certainly for us to know Him, to be loving, to be true, and to be holy. (See Proverbs 11:1; John 13:34; 1 Timothy 2:3–4; 1 Peter 1:16.) That's the general description of what God's will is for all of mankind, but God has individual plans for each person on the earth. God has a special plan for you.

Discovering God's Will

Here are four steps to help you discover God's will for your life:

1. Develop a passionate desire for God and what matters most to Him.

One thing that I've learned is that our hearts' desires must line up with God's perfect will. There was a time when I would get extremely frustrated when things didn't go my way. That frustration came because I didn't have a full understanding that God won't give us whatever we want just because we want it really bad. I had read in Psalm 37:4, "Delight yourself in the Lord, and He will give you the desires of your heart." But I only began to see the results of this word once I understood its true meaning.

This is the powerful lesson that I've learned: we must get to know the heart of God so our hearts' desires line up with His. In my personal prayer time I always pray that God would lead me and guide me in all truth, and that He would inspire me to have thoughts and desires that are pleasing to Him. When you pray this way, God will answer you, and before you know it, you will lose interest in things that you formerly desired. Your desires for certain things will shift. You may even notice that you have a heightened interest in things you never thought you would like.

In Isaiah 43:19 the Lord says, "See, I will do a new thing, now it shall spring forth; shall you not be aware of it? I will even make a way in the wilderness, and rivers in the desert." When you ask God to lead you in His ways, He will do just that. When you trust and acknowledge God, He will direct your path (Prov. 3:5–6). He will show you what matters to Him. Then you will have to choose whether or not you will make the right decision and follow the voice of God.

> We must get to know the heart of God so our hearts' desires line up with His.

2. Spend time praying and reading God's Word.

Spending time praying and reading God's Word is crucial to discovering God's will, because it will help you to recognize His voice. A lot of Christians run to a prophet or pastor to get all the answers. Even though this is a part of seeking counsel, this should not be your first tool for discovering God's will for your life. The Bible says, "Your word I have hidden in my heart, that I might not sin against You" (Ps. 119:11).

Allow the Word of God to be like a seed planted on the inside of you. What is in you is what is going to come out of you. If you have the unquestionable Word of God on the inside of you, the Word of God is going to come out of you.

The Bible says, "Your word is a lamp to my feet and a light to my path" (Ps. 119:105). As you are discovering God's will for your life, praying and hearing God's voice, and reading the Word and being obedient to it will put you in the right position to understand what God's plan is for you.

My daily prayer sounds like this: "Lord, help me to hear Your voice and recognize that it's You, so that I will do the things that You desire of me."

3. Pay attention to your natural gifts and abilities.

When you were born, God gave you gifts. Your gifts are the tools God gave you at birth to serve Him. When you tap into your spiritual gifts, you tap into the special abilities provided by God for building the body of Christ. Your gifts go beyond talent. They are God-given, supernatural abilities.

Some people are waiting for God to answer prayers they have prayed outside of His will for their lives. Don't be the person who waits for a miracle forever because you are trying to function outside the gifts God gave you at birth. (I'll talk more about this later in this chapter when I discuss God's perfect will.)

It is important for you to discover your gifts. Start by taking inventory of what you are good at. These are the things you should focus on. God gives you gifts according to His plans for your life. You have certain gifts because they are what God desires you to have. This must mean He wants you to use those gifts in the area where He needs you to function. When you do this, you are functioning in God's will.

Don't miss God's will by praying for and trying to use gifts God didn't give you. Tap into what God put inside of you to help build His kingdom. That's the will of God for your life.

4. Seek counsel from spiritually mature people.

God places people in our lives to help us. We should not be afraid to seek godly wisdom and counsel when we are confused about God's plan. We can connect with people who are spiritually mature, people who have a relationship with God and will pray on our behalf.

Many times, even though I travel the world evangelizing, I call on those who I know have a relationship with God to help me grasp things I don't understand. The Bible tells us that amongst wise counsel there is safety (Prov. 11:14; 15:22; 24:6). Seek advice from the wise. If you don't have anybody in mind, ask God to connect you with people who will be a blessing to your spiritual walk.

Discovering the will of God is a journey. You need people who are spiritually sound to help you along the way. Don't be prideful and avoid asking for help because you think you can do this thing by yourself. You'll be alone, and you may miss your blessing. Be willing to seek help. Ask questions. Be willing to be mentored. Godly counsel will only push you closer to the discovery of God's perfect will for your life.

Discovering God's will is one thing, but knowing the difference between God's perfect will and His permissive will is the difference between thriving and just surviving in life. I don't know about you, but I want to thrive! So let's learn how prayer can help us discern what part of God's will we are dwelling in. The waiting season is the perfect time for us to get realigned with God.

The Perfect Will

Everything God does is perfect. No doubt about it. God is absolute. God is complete. We should rejoice in the fact that our God is completely free from faults, errors, and defects. So when we think about God's perfect will, we are saying that God's will is faultless. It's a great thing to understand that our waiting is worth it because what we are waiting for is error-free. I believe that an impeccable blessing is worth waiting for. I would rather wait for God's perfect blessing than get in a hurry and receive something flawed. When you receive what you think is a blessing and it has flaws in it, that is proof that it did not come from God. "The blessing of the LORD makes rich, and He adds no sorrow with it" (Prov. 10:22). Anything that comes from God is going to be accurate, precise, and just plain perfect.

It is very important that we know and get in line with God's perfect will. The Bible tells us, "Do not be conformed to this world, but be transformed by the renewing of your mind, that you may prove what is the good and acceptable and perfect will of God" (Rom. 12:2). Your heart's desire should be to live in God's perfect will.

Don't be discouraged, but be aware that there are times when God's will is hidden until it comes to pass. Then there are times when God will reveal His will to us so that we can march along this journey with assurance that everything is going to be all right. God's perfect will can be revealed in prayer, in the Word of God, and in everyday life. God will purposely speak to you or allow things to happen so you can recognize that His perfect will is being done in your life.

Not your will but His

If you are not careful, you can miss God's voice, or even a sign that introduces you to God's perfect will. When we make the assumption that what we see is not God's perfect will because it doesn't look like what we expect it to look like, we place ourselves in danger of missing out on God's flawless plan. Don't ever get in the position of settling for what you want. You have to be dedicated to responding to what God wants. One of the worst things you can do in the waiting season is to make up your own perfect will. When you do this, you automatically disqualify yourself from God's perfect will.

> Some things look better to our eyes, but they are not better for our lives.

It matters deeply to God how we run this race. Your life matters to God. Your heart matters to God. Furthermore, your actions matter to the Lord and reflect Him.

I remember when I wanted to play football in high school. I tried out for the team two years in a row and got cut both years. Pretty embarrassing, right? While I was weeping about being cut from the team two years in a row, I heard God say that football was not His perfect will for my life, but music was. So I went and tried out for the school band. I tried to let music go because being on the football team seemed cooler. That's a lesson in itself.

Some things look better to our eyes, but they are not

better for our lives. When I tried out for the marching band, I was chosen right away. I won awards in our county and across the state of North Carolina. God gifted me from birth to be a musician. I tapped into my gift and was successful.

Failure and defeat are not part of God's perfect plan for our lives. When we are in His perfect will, we are guaranteed great success! Even if I would have made the football team, I probably never would have even played in a game. I may have gotten hurt. I certainly would have been a failure, because that's not what God created me to do. God made it easy for me. I was so flawed at football that God didn't even allow me to make the team. I was angry about this at first, but then I realized it was God's best for me.

> Declare: I choose to live in perfect harmony with God's perfect plan!

What are you working on while you're waiting? Have you ever asked yourself, "Is what I'm praying for a part of God's perfect will for my life?" Pray and ask God to reveal His perfect will for your life. When God reveals His perfect will for your life, it is your responsibility to get in line with it as soon as possible. I mean, you must move quickly. There's an old song I used to hear growing up in church that said the safest place to be is in the will of God.[1]

You have to pray that God's perfect will is being done in your life while you're waiting on God. God's timing is always perfect, but you will only get to see His timing work for you if you are in His perfect will. Otherwise you may find yourself scraping by in God's permissive will.

THE PERMISSIVE WILL

One place I don't ever want to be is in God's permissive will. Some people say they live in God's permissive will. I say that we survive in God's permissive will. God's perfect will is what God desires for our lives. God's permissive will is simply what God allows to happen in our lives. Why would you spend your waiting season surviving in a place that God is just allowing because His perfect will is not being done?

In my view God's permissive will is like a form of punishment. His permissive will may seem like the right thing until our capacity to survive it runs dry. In this place God allows us to have what we prayed for because we refuse to accept what He desires. While you're waiting for your prayers to be answered, it's a good thing to learn to hear from God. You cannot choose to follow your own path. If you do, you're going to be held accountable for doing things your way instead of God's way. The survivalist experience of being in God's permissive will is partly how God holds us accountable for choosing our own path instead of yielding to His ways.

When you don't yield yourself to praying for God's perfect will to be done, you open yourself to God's judgment. And though God's judgment may not kill us in the natural, we will find ourselves slowly dying spiritually. I've been there before. In fact, I'll be transparent with you to help you understand how God permits things to happen even though they are outside of His perfect will.

I had a certain type of woman in mind that I wanted to date. I met a young lady who fit that description. From the outside it seemed as if she possessed every one of my heart's desires. I kept noticing things that were wrong, things that did not line up with what I knew to be God's perfect will for my life. But instead of hearing the voice of God and moving on, I chose to do my own thing. I felt as if I could change her. I thought that I was good enough to make my dreams come true without the help of the Lord.

Even though I knew that relationship wasn't God's will for my life, I ignored the warnings and allowed it to become more serious. That led to major heartache that lasted far too long. I knew that relationship wasn't God's perfect will for me. I knew I was outside the perfect plans God had for my life. But because I wanted to do what I wanted to do, I ended up in God's permissive will.

A lack of patience will cause you to live in God's permissive will instead of His perfect will. God's perfect will is God's pleasure. Stay there. Don't get impatient and end up in God's permissive will, which is man's pleasure.

The good news about God's permissive will is that He can even work that together for your good. He will sometimes allow certain things to happen to test your faith. God will allow some things to happen just to see how faithful you are to Him. Have you ever had a time in your life when you knew God was testing you? Did you pass the test? I hope you can answer yes, but if you answered no, what I'm saying to you today will help you pass from now on.

Realizing that you were just surviving in God's permissive will is certainly a hindrance to receiving the blessings God has in store for you. Don't allow your self-will to be the reason you live in God's permissive will. Be careful not to find yourself being indifferent when it concerns God's plans for your life.

Arrogance is a hindrance. You'll find yourself in God's permissive will before you realize what's happening. Be obedient to the voice of the Lord. Failure to do what God says will place you in God's permissive will. Failure to do what God has already told you to do will just delay your miracle. You already know what God requires of you, so act on it.

By faith you have to trust that what you're believing for from God is certainly on the way. But while you're waiting, you cannot take matters into your own hands. God's permissive will is not a joyful place to live. You will find yourself being happy in His permissive will for a season, thinking that it's His perfect will, then before you know it, you'll be praying for a way of escape. Seek God for His perfect will, and when He reveals it, be obedient to Him.

FINDING PEACE IN THE WAIT

God wants us to thrive during our waiting season, not merely survive, and the only way to do that is to stay focused on His will. I've learned that I cannot wait on God the right way if I decide to focus on my problems and not on my promise. Just when I get excited about my prayers being answered, suddenly a distraction will come. Its purpose is simple: it is meant to throw me off track. But I have found that though I can't keep these distractions from coming, they will only gain the victory if I don't have peace.

To have peace is to be free from disturbance. We all need peace. We all need to be free from all the negative elements that distract us from seeing the blessings of our future. But we don't need just any old kind of peace. We need the peace that only comes from the Lord. This peace is found in the presence of God because He is the one who blocks every trouble.

This time of your life, this waiting season, can be extremely tough. It's easy for a person to be at peace when they are releasing their prayers for a miracle to the Lord. But it gets extremely difficult to maintain that peace when you've been waiting much longer for the miracle than you expected. How many times have you started a journey toward a promise with excitement only to get frustrated after a while because things didn't happen in the way you dreamed? It's in those moments, when you're getting ready to lose your mind and give up on God, that you need His peace.

I have had many moments in my life when I was in dismay over the way my life was rolling along. I just wasn't happy. I knew I possessed the gifts and ability to be a better man, but I couldn't see how my dreams would become my reality. When I had opportunities for advancement come my way, yet those doors ultimately slammed in my face, it was hard for me to remain at peace. Opportunities for relationships, business, financial increase, and ministry kept coming my way, but they would all fail, and I became more and more discouraged. But I eventually found peace.

There were three things I began to do, and as I did, I noticed that the peace of God took over my heart and mind, and I became free from disturbance. These three things will transform your waiting experience.

Praise God in advance.

Praise is a weapon against the stronghold of the enemy. The Bible says, "Out of the mouth of babes and sucklings hast thou ordained strength because of thine enemies, that thou mightest still the enemy and the avenger" (Ps. 8:2, KJV). While I was in my waiting season, I began praising God—not just for what He had already done in my life but also for the miracles I was waiting for. It's called praising God in advance. You see, the absence of peace in your life is caused by the presence of trouble. Praise causes the prince of trouble to flee. When you praise God, your focus is taken off of your struggle, and your attention is put on God.

When you get to your breaking point, dig deep and pull out a praise! Begin to thank God in advance for the miracle you're believing for. His presence will show up, and you'll find yourself free from all the distractions the enemy brought your way. Praise silences the enemy!

Be grateful.

Sometimes we get so caught up thinking about what we want that we end up losing appreciation for what we already have. I believe my toughest moments while waiting on God to answer my prayers came when I thought too long about the future, when I focused on what I wanted to happen instead of on what I'd already been blessed with. Don't make the mistake of creating your own disturbance. There are some negative thoughts we force ourselves to have, and it gets worse when we start speaking words that agree with failure and not the blessings of God.

The apostle Paul said, "I have learned in whatever state

I am to be content" (Phil. 4:11). That is the key to having peace—learning to be content in whatever place you're in. Having gratitude in the midst of your current situation doesn't mean you're going to be in the same place forever. It just means you're willing to accept where you are right now, knowing that the best is yet to come. When you really have the faith to believe that better is coming your way, you too will be free from the disturbances that come to discourage you while you wait on God's best! You will have peace.

Plan for the future.

Naturally you're going to be miserable if you just sit around and mope about the fact that your miracle seems to be taking too long. If you want things to change, you have to do something about it. If you want things to get better, you have to work. In order to work, you must have a plan. If you have a dream, you ask God to give you a plan to see that dream become your reality. I found out that planning for the future can be a stress reliever. After all, one of the greatest signs of your faith is in how you plan for what God promised you. Planning is another way for you to direct your attention away from the disturbances.

You can find peace in your plan. The plan gives you a glimpse of the great things that are coming for you. Whenever God gives me a vision that shows me my blessed future, I feel free from my current reality. Sometimes your current reality can make you feel worthless, but when you decide to plan based on what God has shown you, you will be free from that feeling and God will give you a much better feeling. It's called peace. Don't just sit in misery; pray and ask God to give you a plan—and then work the plan.

The peace of God gives me a calm in my spirit, and it will help you relax in your waiting. God doesn't want you to get comfortable as you wait and stay in the same place forever. But He wants you to remain at peace by staying focused on Him so you will grow through the waiting process.

The Bible tells us, "Be anxious for nothing, but in everything, by prayer and supplication with gratitude, make your requests known to God. And the peace of God, which surpasses all understanding, will protect your hearts and minds through Christ Jesus" (Phil. 4:6–7). God will give you peace in your body, mind, and soul so you can overcome the battle of your mind. And you'll get your joy back. So in your prayer time, don't be afraid to call on "Jehovah Shalom," the Lord our peace. He will show up and deliver you.

PRAY!

Lord, thank You for giving me peace as I stay focused on You. I ask that You would help me to live a life that matches Your perfect will for me. Help me to never be satisfied with my own ways. I pray that You would create a way of escape for me that I may leave Your permissive will and get in line with your perfect will. In Jesus's name, amen.

Now, Declare!

- I will walk in line with God's perfect will for my life (Matt. 6:10).

- I choose to do the will of God, not my own will (John 6:38).

- I will stay in perfect peace as I keep my mind on You (Isa. 26:3).

- I will keep my way pure by living according to God's Word (Ps. 119:9).

- I will persevere so that when I have done the will of God, I will receive what He has promised (Heb. 10:36).

Chapter 5

IT'S ALL ABOUT COMING INTO AGREEMENT WITH GOD

YOU'VE PRAYED. YOU'VE fasted. You've done all you know to do, but you're still waiting for the answer to your prayer. The good news is, even though you're waiting, God has the best answer, simply because God's timing is always perfect and He never fails. If you think now is the time for your prayer to be answered or breakthrough to come, you're wrong. God knows the best time for your answer to be released. Wouldn't you rather trust God than trust yourself? Wouldn't you rather go with God's answer than your own?

Our answers and our timing will always fail. We don't have the understanding or vision needed to independently determine what is right for our lives. God sees through the eyes of eternity. He was there at the foundation of the world. He created us! How could we ever think that our timing is any match for God's?

This is why we should trust in the Lord with all of our

heart. That means trusting His timing, His Word, and His answers. If I trust in the Lord with all my heart, it means I believe that whatever He does is absolutely right. I'm willing to be wrong, knowing that God is always right. Trusting God means that I choose to agree with God and not myself. This is not a matter of agreeing to disagree. When I come into agreement with God, I completely take sides with the perfect One, agreeing that His way, His timing, and His plan are best for my life.

I encourage you to take time today to align yourself with God's Word and His way of doing things. The Bible tells us, "Delight yourself in the LORD, and He will give you the desires of your heart" (Ps. 37:4). As we align with God, our desires will become His desires, our thoughts like His thoughts, and our agendas His agenda. So if God has you in a waiting season, get excited about the fact that He is working in His perfect timing to give just what you need according to His perfect will.

BE ON THE RIGHT TEAM

Back in my childhood days I would meet all my friends at the playground to play basketball. I was a church boy, so I wasn't as athletic as the rest of my friends, but I would still get out there and try to play. One thing that would disappoint me, though, was the process of picking teams. One group would stand on the left, one group would stand on the right, and they would call their team members by name. I was always so disappointed because out of all of the friends who would stand and wait for their name to be called, I was always the last pick for a team. It was never up to me whose team I would be on. I would just have to deal with winning or losing. I can laugh about it now, but I would often end up on the losing team.

As believers we are never God's last choice. You have to see yourself as God's first choice. You may say, "Pastor Marcus, if I am God's first choice, why have I been waiting so long?" It may feel as if everybody else is getting picked for the team while you stand by and wait, as if you are God's last choice. The truth is, you are God's favorite choice. You were born as God's number-one pick. You are on the right team, the winning team, when you agree with God's timing for delivering you into the next season.

You may say, "I don't agree with how God is taking me on this life journey." If that's what you're thinking, you are on the wrong team. If you would rather do things your own way and in your own timing, you're on your own team, and that's not the winning team. Why waste time agreeing with yourself and inadvertently agreeing with the enemy? Why go through life enjoying temporary pleasures on your own team when God has pleasures for you that will last from everlasting to everlasting if you choose His?

Sometimes it looks better to be on another team, but looks can be deceiving. I was taught a long time ago that sometimes the grass looks greener on the other side. Even though this statement is true, it is not until we step on that other grass that we realize our grass was much better. Are you on God's winning team, but you're looking at what others have and trying to join their team? You will lose if you change teams.

I'll admit that one of the hardest things to do while waiting on God's blessing is to watch others be blessed.

Sometimes it's hard to listen to everybody else give their testimony of victory while you sit waiting to testify. It takes strength and maturity to be able to stay in position, knowing that God's best is still being prepared for you. But whatever you do, don't change sides.

In this waiting season you want to win, but you can't be weak and start rushing God. Rushing God is like trying to manipulate Him into releasing your blessing. This is very dangerous. When you're on the right team, it means you're on the winning team. And most of the time the winning team has the best coach. Your coach is God—the One who is perfect in all of His ways, the One who makes no mistakes. It's much like a professional football team. They may lose the first few games of the season, but if they follow the coach, learn the playbook, and are patient, they could win the Super Bowl.

It may feel as if you're losing right now, but trust me, if you are on the Lord's side, you are on the winning side. You are on the right team. Being a part of God's family is one of the greatest positions to be in. Whatever you're waiting for God to do, when you're on the right team, you can believe that you already have it. You can wait and still rejoice, knowing that it's already done. You don't have to wait until the battle is over; when you're on the right team, you can rejoice in advance, knowing that you've already won!

> It may feel as if you're losing right now, but…if you are on the Lord's side, you are on the winning side.

On the Lord's team there are no egos. There is no jealousy. So while you're waiting for your blessing, learn how to celebrate the blessings of your teammates. The Bible says to rejoice with those who rejoice! A good team knows how to celebrate the victory of another teammate because when one wins, they all win.

So don't be down in your waiting season. Get excited about the fact that you are on God's team. Get excited about the fact that you agree with your Coach and whatever He says you'll do, knowing that everything is going to be all right. The enemy's team may get ahead for a while, but it's guaranteed that God's team is going to win.

While you wait, God is giving you strength. He will not let His child suffer. I remember an old song we used to sing in church. The song asked a question, "Where do you stand? Who is on the Lord's side?" Our response to the song was, "I'm on the Lord's side!" While you're waiting, stay on the right team.

WHAT DOES IT MEAN TO AGREE?

Coming into agreement with God is a very important thing. But first we must understand what agreement is. To agree simply means to have the same opinion about something. It means to concur. So a person of faith who trusts God would boldly say, "I completely agree with God about His plans for my life." I want you to declare every day of your life, especially in this waiting season, that you are in harmony with God. You're in full position to agree. The fact that you are believing God right now and trusting Him in this season means you should be rejoicing that incompatibility is upset as it concerns your relationship with God.

One of the things I love about God is that He is

consistent. So when we come into agreement with Him, we can be confident that He's never going to change. God is the same yesterday, today, and forever. Our agreement with God should never change either. When we agree with God, we enter into a binding agreement. This agreement becomes our course of action as we live this journey called life. This means that if God says it's not time for me to receive what I've been praying for, I've already agreed to accept what God allows.

From elementary school to college I always played in the school band, and even since then I've remained involved in music. Playing solo pieces always came easy. I could do my own thing. But when it came time to play as a band, it was very important for everyone to be on the same sheet of music. We had to be in harmony. We had to agree with one another that the selected sheet of music would be the arrangement we all would perform. We had to be in sync in order to sound good.

On some occasions one band member obviously did not agree that the selected sheet of music was the correct one, so he would use his own arrangement of the music. There could have been two hundred band members, but when one band member chose not to play the same sheet of music that the rest of us played, the band would sound horrible.

It's the same way with our lives. It's very important that in your relationship with God you agree to play from the same sheet of music. In the band our sheet music provided the instruction for what our instruments were to play. In life our sheet music is the Scriptures. God's Word was written for us to agree and come into harmony with

God about how to live well. When we choose to make our own arrangements, twisting the Scriptures with our own words, we are choosing to disagree with the Word of God. Don't allow your life to be distorted because you choose to agree with yourself, or even perhaps with the enemy. When you stay in tune with God's plan for your life, the soundtrack of your life will never sound bad, because you are in harmony with our all-knowing God.

Agreement means that you're connected.

When I agree with God, it means that I'm connected with God. No matter what God says, I choose to agree with it, and I'll make arrangements to put myself in the right position to see His promises fulfilled in my life.

I would encourage you to agree with God. Make arrangements to connect with His plans and disconnect from your own plans. Get in harmony with God and His way of doing things.

When you get in agreement with God, you make a decision to coincide with Him. In other words, God and you coexist. When you agree with God, you choose not to fight with God or to come against His plan. You agree to be in sync with the thoughts and plans He has for you.

Agreement is a choice.

God doesn't force you to agree with Him. God simply desires for you to agree with Him. The truth of the matter is, God doesn't need us to agree with Him in order to move. God is going to be God anyway. God is going to cause you to wait on your blessing whether you like it or not. So even if you disagree with God, He will still have His way. Instead of resisting what God is doing in this season of your life, I want you to practice discerning the mind of God concerning you and work on having the same opinion God has about it. Know that because God is perfect in all of His ways, His answer is always guaranteed to be the best answer.

Make no mistake about it—agreeing with God isn't always easy. But it's better for you to agree with God than to agree with the enemy. Sadly, for most of us during this waiting season, our biggest enemy is ourselves. Don't make attempts to please yourself; make your greatest aim to please God. Let your language agree with what God says about your life. Let the way you act show that you agree with God's Word. Be consistent with your actions while you're waiting on God's best. Conform to God's ways and flow with Him. Don't try to make God's plan fit into your plan. Be of the same mind as God. Unite with Him. Even though the waiting is hard, be joyful about agreeing with His plan for your life.

THE CONSEQUENCE OF DISAGREEMENT

One thing I learned in life is that you never tell Mom and Dad no. If my mother or father told me to do something, I was supposed to do it whether I wanted to or not. I imagine that you too can remember those days from your childhood, when you wanted to disagree with your parents or whoever had authority over you, but you didn't because you knew your disagreement would bring serious consequences. It was dangerous for us as children to share our opinion with our parents, especially if it went against their opinions. We quickly learned that if we did not agree with them, they would agree to take the most powerful form of punishment to make sure we knew that there were consequences to disagreeing with them.

The lesson I learned through this was that even though I thought I had a better answer, it was always better for me to agree than to disagree with the ones who were in charge. The ones who are in charge always know what's best, and when we try to override their choice, it is taken as disrespect. There is no honor when we choose to disagree with those we should respect. This powerful lesson that I learned in my early days is the same lesson I apply to my relationship with God today. I don't believe God wants to punish us for disagreeing with Him, but there are consequences to disagreeing with God's plans and directions for our lives.

When you disagree with God, the greatest consequence that you will face is being fooled into believing that all is well when you're actually in the worst position of your life. Here are five other things that will happen if you disagree with God:

1. You will miss the mark of God's perfect timing for your blessing.

2. You will come out of harmony with God.

3. You will miss the benefits of having His clear guidance.

4. You will place yourself in a position of struggling to survive in His permissive will.

5. You will carry unnecessary burdens.

Don't be the person who has an opportunity to live the blessed life and miss it. When you choose to disagree with God, you end up creating your own storms. Don't create your own storm and then expect God to bring you out. Be responsible for your choices. When you are responsible for your choices, you won't have to worry about the consequences of making the wrong decisions, because you will make the right decisions on purpose.

I want to challenge you: if you have been in the position of disagreeing with God, true redemption is available for you right now. You can seize the moment by accepting your current position, knowing that when you get in alignment with God, your past mistakes will not stop your future blessings.

I'm warning you because I don't want you to be surprised by your consequences. I want to motivate you to always agree with God. In the Old Testament, Saul chose to go his own way instead of obeying God, and as a result God rejected him as king of Israel. The Lord told Saul to strike the Amalekites and utterly destroy them, sparing no one and nothing. Saul went down and struck the Amalekites, but instead of destroying everything, he kept some of the sheep and oxen, saying they would be used as sacrifices to God. Yet God wasn't pleased with Saul's actions. He spoke through the prophet Samuel, saying:

> Does the LORD delight in burnt offerings and sacrifices as much as in obeying the voice of the LORD? Obedience is better than sacrifice, a listening ear than the fat of rams. For rebellion is as the sin of witchcraft, and stubbornness is as iniquity and

idolatry. Because you have rejected the word of the LORD, He has also rejected you from being king.

—1 SAMUEL 15:22–23

Saul tried to repent, but it was too late. Samuel told him, "The LORD has torn the kingdom of Israel from you this day, and has given it to a neighbor of yours who is better than you" (1 Sam. 15:28). That neighbor, who would become King David, was "better" than Saul because he was a man after God's own heart, one who would agree with God and choose to stay in sync with Him (Acts 13:22).

It's so true. You have the freedom to make whatever decisions you want to make, but you are not free to choose your own consequences. Don't end up on the wrong side of God's blessing because you choose to take matters into your own hands. Agree with the One who is in control. God is in control.

AGREEING WITH THE WORD OF GOD

The Bible tells us that the Word of God is a lamp to our feet and a light to our path (Ps. 119:105). One of the greatest benefits of being a child of God is that God Almighty gives us clear guidance in life. There will never be a time in life when God will purposely cause us to be confused. Confusion is not of God. The devil is the author of confusion. (See 1 Corinthians 14:23.) Moreover, we know that the devil is not in control.

Sometimes we find ourselves following our own desires and not following the Word of God. Our own desires can be confusing, but the Word of God is always firm. When God speaks, He makes no mistakes. We also know that, according 2 Corinthians 1:20, the promises of God are yes and amen. In other words, if God makes a promise, it must come to pass. This is another reason it is so important for us to agree with God and His Word. God's Word will never return void (Isa. 55:11).

God made promises concerning your life in His Word. Even in the middle of this waiting season you can remain joyful because you know what God promised you and that everything is going to be all right. Why do you know this? Because God's Word is true and must come to pass. He does not want you to be confused, so He speaks to you. It is your responsibility to listen to His Word, agree with His Word, and respect the power of His Word.

You cannot follow your own words, because your own words come with tainted ambition. The real power is in God. There is limitless power in God's words.

Sometimes when referring to God we call Him God Almighty. The name Almighty references God's unlimited power, and the same power that rests in His name rests in His words. So when we agree with God, we also agree with His words.

The question I want to ask you is this: What has God said about you lately? What is He speaking to your heart about your situation? You may say, "Pastor Marcus, I have no idea what God is saying concerning my situation." Let me tell you, there is great joy when you can hear the voice of God. His words give us assurance. When God speaks, He confirms His promises over our lives. When we speak to ourselves concerning our situation with no backing from the Word of God, we can get confused. We have so many ideas about what should be that we often miss the answer God has for us. When God speaks our answer, our situation is immediately simplified.

One of the most powerful things about God's Word is that it enlightens us. God's Word gives us greater knowledge and understanding about where we are in life. God's Word has the power to give us spiritual knowledge or insight about everything concerning our lives. When God speaks a word to us, He informs us and makes us aware of how He's preparing His best for us while we wait.

I want to encourage you to get in agreement with God's Word, because His Word has the power to change your situation. When God speaks a word of healing, healing has to take place. Psalm 107:20 says, "He sent His word and healed them and delivered them from their destruction." When God speaks a word of restoration, restoration has to take place. When God speaks a word about your finances breaking through, your finances will increase. God has power in His mouth, and so do you! The Bible tells us that "death and life are in the power of the tongue" (Prov. 18:21). That means if the Word of God lives in us, we to have the power to speak the Word and watch things come to pass.

What words are you speaking over yourself while you wait? I want to challenge you right now: don't you dare agree with the enemy and speak words against your future blessings. Get in agreement with God and speak His Word over your life and your future. Your words can either inspire you or destroy you. God's Word will destroy the enemy's plans against your life. His words inspire you and push you to the next level. So be careful with your words.

Also, in this season of waiting, make sure you don't focus on trusting the words of man. Purposely trust the words of God. God will not be silent when it concerns you. During this waiting season God will speak to you and confirm His promises as you seek Him in prayer.

Here's how I know God's words have power. When I was twenty-six years old, I was faced with a dangerous situation. I was so nervous because I didn't know what the outcome would be. In my heart and mind I expected the worst to take place. I went to breakfast with my grandmother so I could talk and share my heart with her. As I was talking, I began to cry in fear. Once I finished crying and telling my grandmother my story, she told me that at that very moment God had spoken to her and told her everything was going to be all right. At first I didn't believe her. I was so used to everybody always saying the same thing. But sure enough, a few weeks later, I found out that the word God spoke to my grandmother concerning my situation was true. It was so real. Everything was all right.

I believe right now that everything you're worried about, God is going to make right. You've been waiting and worrying, but God's Word says, "Those who wait upon the LORD shall renew their strength" (Isa. 40:31). I declare that your waiting season is making you stronger.

Let God speak His Word over your life. His words have power.

GET ON BOARD

I have the wonderful opportunity to travel the world and share God's good news with so many people. As a part of my journey, I get the chance to fly a lot. In the airports while waiting I always eagerly anticipate the gate agent calling our flight number and declaring that it's almost time to leave. If you fly or travel a lot, you understand how aggravating it is to wait for that special call. Sitting in the airport is tiring. Let's not forget about the TSA checkpoint that we have to pass through in order to get to our appropriate gate.

So after all that, what great joy it is when they announce that my flight is ready to leave. Not many people will sit in the airport that long, finally get the call that it's time to board, and then purposely avoid boarding. It doesn't make any sense. Even though the waiting can make us uncomfortable, when we hear that call to board the plane, we get up because it's time to move and get on board. We may not agree with having to wait so long for the flight, but we do agree that when it's time to go, it's time to go!

This scenario reminds me of how it is when we're waiting on God to move. Yes, waiting gets aggravating sometimes. It's frustrating, especially knowing that we've been waiting longer than we ever expected for the answers

> Declare: I will not agree with the negative voices in the world; I will only agree with God!

to our prayers to be manifested in our lives. Even though we don't always agree with the length of our waiting season, we must agree that God's timing is perfect. When God calls us to get on board, we have to agree that if it took this long, it must have been meant to be. When God says it's time to go, I don't care how frustrated you are with the amount of time that you've been waiting on the call, the best thing you can do is accept the blessing and get on board. You have to get in agreement with God quickly.

There is no sense in going back and forth with God

about His boarding time or how long it is taking Him to release His blessings. If we do, we may miss the blessing. I think of it this way: If I go to an airport and, right as it is time to board the plane, I start arguing with the gate agent that, according to my calculations, the boarding process is taking too long, I run the risk of having the door shut on me and missing my flight.

How much fussing have you done with God? How often do you argue with God about His schedule for your life? Let me warn you: if you spend time arguing with God because you're tired of waiting, God may shut the door on your blessing. Back to the airport scenario: if I get mad because I feel as though I've waited too long for my flight and argue with the gate agent while the flight is boarding, I risk missing that flight and having to wait even longer for another flight to take me to my destination.

The same thing can happen between you and God. If you miss your blessing because you refuse to get on board when God says it's time for you to board, you'll be stuck in the same position, waiting longer than you waited before. Why put yourself through that torment? Why not just get on board? I've said it so many times in this book, but I'll say it again: God's timing is always perfect! Stop complaining. The more you draw closer to God, the more you'll understand His voice and His call. When God calls your name, don't hesitate to move.

I want to encourage you to start preboarding now. To preboard as it concerns your waiting season is to prepare your mind in advance for the release of the blessing. My grandfather would always tell me, "You've got to see it before you see it, or you never will see it." Start agreeing with God now. Imagine yourself living in the blessing of God now.

Don't miss your moment because you're focusing on the negative aspects of your waiting season. When you focus more on the negative, you will be so focused on the wrong things that you miss out on the right things.

Don't miss your flight! Get on board with what God wants to do now so you can receive His blessings at the right time. When God says it's time to go, agree with Him and get on board. When God calls you to make a move, the best thing you can do is get out of your own way. Don't agree with what you think is right; agree with God's perfect timing. When God calls you to get on board, you should be so excited about His call to make a move that you rejoice, knowing that your waiting wasn't in vain.

Obedience: The Ultimate Sign of Agreement

One of the clearest ways we show that we are in agreement with God is by obeying Him. To be obedient to God simply means that we are in compliance with His orders, requests, or laws. When we are obedient to God, it means we are submitted to His authority. It is a safe practice to be obedient to God. It is a wise practice to make yourself compliant with God's will, to submit to God's every wish and command concerning your life.

I want to encourage you to refuse to accept anything without God's approval. When you agree with God, it's your way of saying, "I'm unwilling to agree with anything other than that which agrees with God and His Word."

Obedience accepts what God wants. Obedience will cause you to move according to God's plan.

When you are obedient to God's instructions, you enable God to place you in the perfect position to receive the greatest blessings of your life. God told Abraham to leave his family and the land he knew and go to a place he knew not. Abraham could have argued with God or asked Him for clearer directions, but he didn't do that. He packed up his belongings and left. (See Genesis 12.) In this new land God made Abraham an exceedingly wealthy man, but more importantly God made him the father of the great nation of Israel. Had he remained where he was, who knows how many blessings Abraham would have missed. An obedient child of God will not protest God's will. He will accept it, knowing that God's plans for us are good.

Obey, even when it doesn't make sense.

Sometimes we don't understand why we are obeying God, but it is possible to be obedient without understanding why. Noah built an ark to prepare for a flood when it had never even rained (Gen. 6:9–22). But because of his obedience, he and his family were saved.

We don't always know why God does what He does, but we show our faith and trust in God when we obey Him without knowing why. We must trust in the almighty God so much that even when we don't understand what He's telling us to do, we still know how to agree with Him. We can obey based on what we do know, which is that God is perfect in all His ways and He has already prepared the way for us.

If God gives us an instruction, it is in our best interest to do exactly what He says to do. If we choose to disobey His guidance, we will find ourselves at crossroads and dead ends, lost and unable to find our way.

Surrender to God.

In a nutshell, obedience is total surrender to God. Have you totally surrendered to God yet? Is this waiting season a struggle because you haven't totally surrendered to God? If this is the case, you can surrender to God right now. Your waiting season does not have to be any harder than it is. You can choose to submit to God's will, get on board with His plan, and walk in faithful obedience to His purpose for your life. If you do, you will open your life up to a whole new realm of blessing. Let's take a moment and explore how obedience blesses even a season of waiting.

The benefits of obeying God

1. Obedience keeps you in position to be blessed.

2. Obedience helps you to become more like our heavenly Father.

3. Obedience causes you to gain knowledge and wisdom.

4. Obedience encourages you to grow spiritually.

5. Obedience positions you to see God's promises fulfilled.

Obedience proves your love for God.

When you truly love God, obedience is not a burden. Jesus said, "If you love Me, keep My commandments....If a man loves Me, he will keep My word. My Father will love him, and We will come to him, and make Our home with him. He who does not love Me does not keep My words" (John 14:15, 23–24). Those who obey God receive the love of God.

One of the greatest acts of faith you can perform during your waiting season is to obey God's instructions. Don't wait to be obedient; be obedient now. Even when you find yourself waiting for God to bless you, if you are not obedient to His Word, you will wait longer for your blessing than originally intended.

When it comes to agreeing with God during the waiting season, obedience is required. See God's commands as a blessing. When you see God's orders as a means through which He wants to bring blessing in your life, you will not be bound by God's orders. Trust and obey, because it's your key to freedom.

There have been many times in my ministry when God has told me to do something and I didn't understand why. One of the biggest mistakes I've ever made in ministry was to disobey the voice of God.

Disobeying God or trying to rush the blessing and make things happen ourselves will cause us to struggle unnecessarily. I've determined to never reject God's instructions and do my own thing again. I know from experience that it doesn't work out well.

When you are disobedient, you may not experience the consequences right away, but after a while your disobedience will catch up to you. That is why I always encourage believers to agree with God. Remember this: faith, prayer, and obedience come first, then God opens the door for you to be blessed. When we are obedient, I believe it speaks volumes to God. Our obedience and agreement with God are the outward evidence that we truly trust in the Lord with all of our hearts and are nearing readiness to handle what's on the other side of the wait.

PRAY!

Father, I thank You for teaching me how to agree with You. Help me to live a life that is in agreement with Your ways and not the enemy's. I will not lose, because I'm on Your team. Help me to know Your voice and agree with You, in Jesus's name, amen.

NOW, DECLARE!

- I will not agree with the negative elements in my life; I take every negative thought captive to the obedience of Christ (2 Cor. 10:5).

- I will speak words that agree with the blessings of my future (Ps. 19:14).

- Because I agree with God, I will spend my waiting days in peace (Job 22:21).

- I will run this race with patience, and I will win because I'm on the right team (Heb. 12:1–2).

- I declare that all the words the Lord has spoken over my life, I will do (Exod. 24:3).

PART II

HOW TO EMBRACE
GOD'S TIMING

Chapter 6

GOD'S TIMING FOR DISCOVERING YOUR PURPOSE

LL OF US have a purpose in life. The truth of the matter is, we are not here by mistake, because God makes no mistakes. God had a special reason for creating each of us, and the life He gave us is full of purpose. A lot of people go through life wondering what their purpose is. I hope to help clear that up in this chapter, because I believe the worst thing any human being can do is live their life without ever discovering their God-given purpose.

There are so many people in graveyards all around the world who never discovered their purpose—what they were born to do, why they were created to live. If you can discover your purpose, waiting won't be so hard. What if you've been waiting so long to win because God is waiting for you to discover your purpose? What if God is waiting to deliver your miracle because you are living outside of His purpose for your life and He doesn't want you to waste

His blessing doing the wrong thing? This is why it's very important for you to understand God's perfect timing for you to walk in your purpose. Here is what I understand about mine.

I was born on October 11, 1986, in a place called Poughkeepsie, New York. It's right up the Hudson River. At the time of my birth my mother was fifteen and my father was seventeen. Many people would have assumed that my birth was a mistake because I was born to such young parents, but I assure you, that was not the case.

My grandparents were in the room when I was born, and I've heard that my grandfather prayed for me less than thirty seconds after I came out of the womb. He laid hands on me and declared that my life would be blessed. God has brought that word to pass. God is still not through with me yet, but I know that the blessings on my life are because of that moment. The man of God prayed for me and spoke blessings over my life. Even though my mother was a teenager who was judged by her church, that didn't change the fact that my life had purpose.

You may have been born to a single parent. You may have been adopted. Throughout your life, you may have felt as though you're not supposed to be here. I don't believe anybody is on this earth by accident. I believe all of us were born for a reason. Furthermore we were all born for a very good reason. There is something that only you can accomplish in the world. It is your responsibility to discover that purpose. It is your responsibility to accept the assignment God has on your life so you can see His purpose fulfilled. You were born into this world not to waste space and time but to accomplish great exploits for the glory of God.

Your birth was the day you began your assignment in this world. See your birthday as you at the starting line on a mission to reach the finish line, and as long as you are alive, you are still running the race. Your purpose is discovered while you run this race called life. Every time I get discouraged while I'm running this race, I begin to declare out loud that I am born to win; I am born to succeed. I begin to declare that my life is not a waste. My life is a win.

When you were born, God was bringing forth something great that the world had never seen before. You just have to be patient enough to allow it to manifest. You must accept the fact that God never would have created you if He intended to waste you. That is your responsibility. You are a blessing to this world, so be willing to wait so God can develop the best in you. If you'll find the patience to wait on God, you will win.

WHAT IS PURPOSE?

Oftentimes people like me encourage people like you to discover their purpose. We get them all excited about walking in their purpose. Then after they've stopped shouting, they say, "Well, what is purpose?" Let me answer that for you. Purpose is the reason for which something is done or created, a reason something exists. So when you discover the reason you were born, you have actually discovered your purpose. I get excited when I think about the fact that God had a specific intention or objective for creating me. God Almighty actually took time to prepare me for this world. He did the same for you. God placed within you everything you need to accomplish His intentions for you.

You never have to wonder if you have the tools necessary to fulfill your God-given purpose. When you were born, you had everything you needed to walk in your purpose with excellence. Your purpose is the reason God made you. Your birth was not a coincidence. There was a reason you had to be born. The reason may be hidden or sometimes not so obvious, but this is why you have to understand your responsibility to discover it and walk in it. Every so often I think that God doesn't necessarily need us. God is almighty. God is all-powerful. God is everywhere at the same time. God really doesn't need us. He doesn't need any help.

Declare: My life is not a waste. My life is a win.

It doesn't hurt my feelings to know that God doesn't need me. I get excited about the fact that God simply desires me. God created you because He desires you. God couldn't wait for you to be born so that you could fulfill His purpose for your life. So when you discover your purpose, you discover the reason God desires for you to exist. That's powerful to think about. If you have been struggling with self-esteem in any way, your self-esteem struggle should end right now. After reading how powerful you are, that God actually desires you and has a purpose for you, you should get excited about life.

It is key that you realize that the purpose of your life is for you to discover your gift. You should be working to develop and perfect your gifts so you can share them with the world. Purpose has nothing to do with being happy all the time. But it does have a lot to do with you helping others experience happiness and true joy.

To discover my purpose, I had to first find what I was passionate about. In time I realized that I was passionate about encouraging and uplifting others. In that I realized that my purpose was to bless people.

What are you passionate about? While you are waiting on God to cause you to walk fully in your purpose, do what you're passionate about. Ask yourself this question: "When I leave this earth, what do I want to be remembered for?" The answer to that question will lead you to your purpose.

Every day our lives are changing. Our relationships change. Our work changes. There are even changes that take place inside of us. There's nothing wrong with change, but as we are discovering and living out our purpose while waiting on God, there are some things that we need to do. Life is full of creativity. Get creative while discovering your purpose.

Do something that you've never done before. Ask God to do a new thing in you so that you won't be stuck in the same place forever. Your purpose is about more than you doing what makes you comfortable. You have to step up and step out. Let the warm joy and love of God become a part of your life. Take time to focus on helping others. Whatever you do, don't try to duplicate somebody else's purpose. Just be yourself. Listen to the voice of God and allow Him to lead you and guide you in your purpose. God wants you to live out your purpose to the fullest, to experience the utmost of life, to have a fresh experience of the good life every single day.

Two of the best parts of your life are the day you are born and the day you realize why you were born. Of course, the day you accept Jesus Christ as your personal Savior is the greatest day of your life, and that just adds to the joy of discovering your purpose because you will now be able to live out your purpose to the glory of God. Your purpose is the reason you cannot waste time with the wrong people or doing things that don't make you better. The world needs what God has placed within you. That is why it's so important that you discover your purpose.

As you're reading this book, you should be motivated to find out why you are alive. When you were born, your birth certificate didn't tell you why you were born. But the fact that you are alive is proof that God has an assignment for you. You must fulfill your purpose. God's timing is perfect as it pertains to your purpose being fulfilled. Don't rush this. Take your time and allow God to mold you and make you into the person He created you to be. He created you with intentions—good intentions. God took the time to form you in your mother's womb and breathe life into you. (See Psalm 139.) That alone should tell you that your purpose is great.

Don't Walk in the Wrong Purpose

Proverbs 16:9 tells us that "a man's heart devises his way, but the Lord directs his steps." I learned this lesson early in life. When I was in middle school and high school, I tried out for two sports teams. I tried out for the basketball team when I was in the eighth grade, and I tried out for the football team when I was in the ninth and tenth grades. Both tryout experiences were unsuccessful. I wanted to be an athlete so badly. Growing up, my parents and grandparents would buy me basketball and football collectors' cards. I would watch videos of professional athletes. I loved hearing their stories and seeing the reaction they would receive when they scored a touchdown or made the winning basket. I wanted that dream to come true for me. But every year I tried out, I got cut from the team.

I can laugh about those experiences now, but while it was happening, I was heartbroken. I really thought I was good enough to play sports. I thought that by watching sports videos and collecting sports cards and even playing sports in the neighborhood with my friends I would be prepared to start my athletic career. It all failed. In fact, when I was in tenth grade, I was the only student who got cut from the football team that year. Can you imagine how I felt? I watched everybody else make the team except me.

At that moment, I realized that playing sports was not my purpose. Playing sports was my dream because it looked cool on others. Sports didn't look cool on me at all. I had to find my purpose. After getting cut from the football team, I decided to return to what I loved doing when I was a child—playing instruments.

I was born with the ability to hear music and then communicate it on an instrument. I never took piano or drum lessons. I couldn't even read music early on. But I had a natural gift to hear a sound and then be able to duplicate that sound for the listening pleasure of others. I tapped into what I was born to do and decided to embrace what God gave me at birth. I was born with the ability to communicate, both verbally as a speaker and musically. I was able to join the high school band. I was accepted quickly. I learned the music within hours, and I became a section leader in the marching band. I played the drums in the marching band, and I also joined the jazz band playing jazz piano. I was so good at it that I won multiple awards locally, countywide, and statewide. My musical abilities opened the door for me to go to college on a jazz scholarship. I was a successful musician even at an early age.

I'm telling you this story not to brag about my musical accomplishments but to encourage you to tap into what you were born to do. Do not waste time chasing a dream that is not for you. In fact, I don't even like to tell people to chase their dreams. I believe that your dreams are your dreams, so you don't have to chase them because they're already a part of you. So many of us have wasted time trying to accomplish things in life that God did not create us to do. Your waiting season is going to be extended if you find yourself wanting a miracle that doesn't belong to you. I would encourage you not to drain yourself running after answers that aren't for you.

Can you imagine what would have happened to me if I had continued to pursue sports even though it was not God's plan for me to become an athlete? What if I had tried out for the team the next year and the next year? I never would have had the opportunity to join the music department in my school, have a successful musical ride, or even go to college on a jazz band scholarship. I hope you understand my explanation here. This is why I'm so motivated to help you stop wasting time doing things that don't draw you closer to your destiny.

As I said before, you have to discover what flows out of you naturally. You have to discover the gifts God gave you at birth. I want you to use this waiting time to check on your automatic abilities. Don't allow others to convince you that you should be doing something more interesting when you know that what God gave you to do is the greatest assignment of your life. Don't do as I did in my early age and just flow with the waves of popularity. You have to flow with the waves of your purpose. When you flow with the waves of your purpose, failure will never be an option. You won't get cut from the team when you operate in your purpose.

Don't forfeit the success God has for you by forfeiting your God-given purpose. Wasting time chasing someone else's dream will put you in position to miss out on the blessed results God has for you. Get in agreement with God and fall in love with your purpose. Even if what you do is not necessarily the popular thing to do, it's the right thing for you to do. The Bible tells us that our obedience is better than sacrifice. You must realize that when you step out of God's plan for your life and try to accomplish your own plan, you're walking in disobedience. The last thing I want is to try to be something or somebody God did not create me to be.

You're waiting and waiting and wanting to win, but you'll never win if you don't stay in your lane. You may do some things and it may seem as though you are winning, but your winning experience will only be temporary when you're outside of God's purposeful plan for your life. Don't be like me and chase after the wrong destiny. You will never make the team. You will always get cut. You will always walk in failure until you say yes to the Lord and get in line with what He has for you. Don't pursue the wrong purpose. Do what God gave you to do, and success will be your only destination. It's not about what we want; it's about what God wants for us.

TAKE TIME TO DEVELOP

Growth and development are two things we should be focused on while we're waiting on God. Focusing on the answer is great. Focusing on the miracle is awesome. But what's better is to focus on what will draw us closer to our answers. What are you doing while you wait? Whenever I'm between my prayer and the answer to my prayer, I ask God to help me to develop and grow. There are some things in life that we ask God for that He will not release to us until we have matured well enough to receive them. God is not a wasteful God. He will only release things to us if we are prepared to receive them. Maturity is one of the greatest gifts God gives. Unfortunately there are a lot of people who have a big prayer request list, but they haven't matured. God will not release certain blessings into their life because they are not mature enough to handle them.

I like to say that maturity is proof of growth and development. The Bible says in 1 Corinthians 14:20, "Brothers, do not be children in your thinking; rather be infants in evil, but in your thinking be mature." Are you using this waiting season to grow and develop your gift? Are you using this waiting season to mature and draw closer to God? If so, you are on the right track. In order to fulfill your God-given purpose the right way, you have to allow yourself to develop, grow, and mature. Without development, growth, or maturity, you will not be able to handle the magnitude of the blessing God is sending your way. You have to grow up in the spirit. In fact, you have to grow into your purpose. One way to get through your waiting season is to understand that fast growth is never any good. We live in a microwave type of society. Most of my generation wants things quick, fast, and in a hurry. You don't meet many people who want to take their time to develop into their purpose.

The Lord gave me a statement that I often use to help people be patient: slow growth is better than no growth. Waiting on God takes us being able to understand that some things are released to us as a part of a slow process. But we have to be thankful for the slow process. It's in the slow process that we develop. Development simply means to grow and become more advanced. Development is a good thing. Development doesn't hurt you; development helps you. Development births expansion. While I wait, I want to be developing and expanding.

One thing that God loves from us as His children is our appreciation for His developing us. Perhaps the person you were five years ago wouldn't be able to wait with the level of joy that you're waiting with now. That is a sign of growth. I believe that even now God is increasing your wisdom. God is also increasing your patience.

I have to be honest with you about something: patience has been a struggle of mine for a long time. God had to take me through a tough process for me to understand that patience really is a virtue. I used to be the type of person who expected quick results. It wasn't until I experienced the detriment of quick results that I began to appreciate

God's process. Even though the development process can be slow, I still appreciate it.

Discovering your purpose is a process. You have to grow toward your destiny. Don't just go toward your destiny, but grow toward your destiny. As you take time to develop, you'll learn more about how to successfully fulfill your God-given purpose. This is a fact. God's timing is always perfect when it comes to discovering your purpose. He knows the exact amount of time you need to grow and develop before He releases His best to you.

Your success is defined by your personal growth. If you don't allow yourself to grow and develop, you will not allow yourself to be successful. But developing is not always a pleasurable experience. Most of our growth and development takes place when we experience pain.

It's just like athletes working out in the gym. They work hard and they feel pain, but the hard work and the pain are proof that they had a good workout. They always say at the gym, no pain, no gain! I would say the same to you as it concerns your waiting experience and your purpose. No pain, no gain! I know this to be a fact. If it wasn't for the pain that I experienced even within the last ten years of my life, I would not be able to write this book and encourage you at this level. The pain of my past did nothing but prepare me for my purpose. My past did not define me. It put me in the right position to learn and grow into the person God wanted me to be.

Some people never grow. You must make sure that you

> Declare: Every day I take another step closer to my destiny!

surround yourself with people who love development and growth. You will always be stuck in the same place if you surround yourself with people who have no desire to grow or mature. Get around people who are excited about growth. Get around people who are motivated to discover their purpose and walk in it with excellence. If you stay next to people who have grown and developed, they can help you to grow and develop as well.

Connect with people who are in places that you want to go. While you're waiting on God to release the blessing in your life, those people will help you to mature. But remember, it takes time. Slow growth is better than no growth at all. Take your time and allow God to develop you the right way. I promise you will be prepared to receive God's best for you.

MOVING TOO FAST?

My grandfather has always said to me, "Slow down, Marcus." As you might imagine, I was being told to slow down because I wanted things to move fast. There's nothing like the feeling of excitement that comes when God answers your prayers. It's a great feeling when you have big dreams and you feel as though they will become a reality. When talking about how God has perfect timing for a purpose, it is very important that I encourage you not to move too fast. I'll tell you why by sharing another portion of my testimony. Ministry hasn't always been so great for me. There was a time in my life when I wasn't sure whether I should keep going or quit.

My struggle had nothing to do with me discovering my purpose; it had everything to do with me stepping into my purpose too soon. I always knew that God wanted me to become a pastor. Even at a young age I would preach the gospel and people would get saved. I would pray for the sick and their bodies would be healed. I would invite people to my crusades and hundreds would come. I felt as if I should become a pastor because I was getting such great results, but I moved too fast. I started a church in Connecticut in an elementary school cafeteria. We had ten people on the first day. Within a year we had sixty people attending.

I got excited about how the church was growing and that everyone seemed to be so happy at my church, so I started preparing for bigger things. We were in a really good season, but then suddenly things changed. All of a sudden it was as if things turned for the worse. Unfortunately I had to close the doors of the church. I was heartbroken. I was a little embarrassed but more heartbroken because the dream that I expected to become my reality didn't work out.

During that season God had called me to be an evangelist and not a pastor. I thought that because I was able to gather people into churches, preach the gospel, and see them get saved and healed, I was supposed to start a church and become a pastor. I was wrong. Perhaps God will have me pastor a church at some point in the future, but I moved too fast in that season. I know that my purpose is to pastor people, but I stepped into that purpose out of God's perfect timing and it failed. I'm in a season right now where God wants me to be an author and evangelist, but I was trying to be the pastor of a church. All of these things are a part of my true purpose, but I didn't pursue them all in God's perfect timing.

Are you doing some things that you know are a part of your purpose but that you're not supposed to be walking in right now? If you know you've been called to complete certain God-given assignments but you're not seeing the fruit of your assignment, it may be because you're out of sync with God's timing. Don't move too fast. Don't do things that you know are right in the wrong season. You won't get the right results, and you'll end up carrying unnecessary burdens.

Let God do the work in you. If you don't, you will end up blocking your blessings because you're moving too quickly. Just as all great things take time, the perfection of your God-given purpose will take time. Don't get weary in your well-doing and try to make things happen yourself. The Bible says in due season you shall reap if you faint not (Gal. 6:9). When we do things in our own timing, moving too fast, we tell God that we don't need Him and that our plan is better than His plan.

Your waiting season won't last forever. Learn to make the best of this moment. Learn to develop and grow in this season. Growing and developing is a part of your purpose. Moving too fast will cause you to miss out on lessons that you need to learn. Moving too fast may cause you to miss your blessing. It's almost like a person driving too fast on their way to a place they've never been to before. They can have a map in front of them or they could be using GPS, but if they are moving too fast they can miss the destination. Moving too fast can be dangerous. You may miss out on a warning sign or collide with another vehicle. Don't miss your destination because you're moving too fast.

God is leading you and guiding you during this waiting season. If you are moving too fast, you could end up journeying right past your destination. You could even put yourself in spiritual danger and have a head-on collision with the enemy. Certainly you don't want to get lost and end up going back to your past. So as my grandfather told me, slow down; take your time; don't move too fast. It's a good thing to be in the waiting season. Don't be in such a hurry to cut out of it. You may miss the key elements you need to be able to enjoy your blessing when it arrives. Take your time and discover your purpose. Relax. God is not going to allow you to miss your blessing if you are doing the right thing while waiting.

PRAY!

Lord, I thank You for causing me to discover my purpose. Help me to never be confused about my assignment in life. Your timing is perfect for my purpose to be fulfilled. I will be a success in Jesus's name, amen.

NOW, DECLARE!

- My purpose is great, and it will be fulfilled because my God will equip me with every good thing to do His will (Heb. 13:20–21).

- My birth was not a mistake; I am fearfully and wonderfully made (Ps. 139:14).

- God's plan for my life includes an amazing purpose that will glorify Him (Jer. 29:11).

- I will not start and quit; I will start and finish (Phil. 3:14).

- I will be strong and I will not give up, for my work will be rewarded (2 Chron. 15:7).

Chapter 7

GOD'S TIMING FOR YOUR RELATIONSHIPS

THE BEST RELATIONSHIP a human being can have is a real relationship with God. This is a powerful statement. When human beings come to understand that the best relationship they could ever have is with God, their lives will never be the same again. I often think about the promise God made to Joshua. As God was sending Joshua to lead the children of Israel into the Promised Land, God told Joshua that He would never leave him nor forsake him (Deut. 31:6). I get excited when I read that passage of Scripture, because I know the promise God made to Joshua is the same promise He makes to you and me.

The good news about your life as a believer in Jesus is that God will never ever leave you to live this life alone. You are not in this thing by yourself. While you are waiting on God to turn your situation around or to release a miracle in your life, you may be feeling extremely lonely.

But today can be the last time you feel alone. You have an opportunity to embrace the best relationship ever. Your relationship with God is the greatest connection you could ever have, one that can never be broken, and you never have to question whether or not it's real. There is such a thing as false friendships, but there is nothing false about God. Your relationship with Him is real and powerful.

When you embrace a relationship with God the right way, it changes your life. God is able to blow your mind with His love, but only if you let Him. While you are waiting on God's best for you, you have to build your relationship with Him. You cannot endure this waiting season all alone. The truth of the matter is, God has graced you with great power, but you aren't God. You have wisdom, but you don't have as much wisdom as God has. You think you know what you need, but God has a better understanding of what you need. Furthermore, He has a better understanding of the right timing for you to receive His best for you.

While you are waiting to win, why not embrace the fact that the almighty God wants to have a real relationship with you? Don't miss out on this great connection. You never have to wonder whether God loves you, and you never have to question His desire to bless you. Even while you're waiting on your earthly relationships to develop or become stronger, you can also allow your relationship with God to grow stronger. Imagine this: your earthly relationships are not working out but your godly relationship is getting better and better. I love a song that many worship teams around the country sing. It's called "Chasing After You." This song is so powerful because it reminds us of how we should be pursuing God daily—that we should be chasing after Him.

Developing a real relationship with God starts with prayer, which opens the door for you to hear Him clearly. I always say one of the best benefits of being a child of God is the ability to receive clear guidance from Him. There are so many people who are confused about life, and one of the most confusing seasons of life is when we are in a waiting season. You don't have to be confused about which direction to go while you wait. When you have a relationship with God, you have the benefit of His clear guidance.

One of the prayers I pray daily is this: "Lord, lead me and guide me. Help me to hear Your voice and be obedient to Your instructions so I will always be in the perfect position to receive from You and be used by You." When I began to pray that prayer, I noticed that I was able to recognize the voice of the Lord so clearly. I noticed that I was no longer confused and that I began to walk confidently. Why? I was walking to the beat of God's voice.

My relationship with God is the reason I am able to live with such confidence. You must get to the place where you recognize that your wait is about your building a stronger relationship with the Lord. Before you ask God to build up your earthly relationships, you must first ask Him to bless your relationship with Him. The relationship you have with yourself is very important, but it's not more important than your relationship with God. The relationship you have with others here on the earth is very important, but it's not more important than your relationship with God. Your relationship with God is the most important relationship, and His desire is to draw you closer to Himself.

Broken Relationships

One of the things we have to deal with in life is failure. Even though we may like to decree and declare that failure is not an option, we need to be honest about the fact that failure does happen. None of us look forward to failure, but when failure does happen, what do we do next? At least if we understand that failure does take place, when it happens we won't be so shocked and it won't affect us in such a negative way. I have learned that relationships do fail. There is such a thing as broken relationships.

I said previously that the best relationship a human being can have is a relationship with God. In talking about our relationship with God, I specifically pointed out that a real relationship with God can never be broken. This is true as it pertains to how we connect with God, but it is not a guarantee that our relationships with other human beings will never be broken. Broken relationships are real, and you must know how to get through the experience of a broken relationship.

God shuts some doors in our lives to bless us. Resist the temptation to return to places you've been delivered from.

Friendships break. Romantic relationships break. Even family relationships can become fractured. Perhaps you're reading this book and you are waiting for God to heal a relationship in your life. You want God to restore your friendships, or perhaps you are praying for your marriage to be restored. I've been through this, to be waiting for answers regarding your relationships. It's a tough season to get through, but you can get through it. God will not let you stay broken about this thing forever. Broken relationships are extremely heavy burdens to carry.

Have you ever been stabbed in the back? I have, and it's not a good feeling. Sometimes it takes a long time to get over the pain of a broken relationship. I remember when I was in middle school in Germany and my fifth-grade girlfriend broke my heart. I often laugh about it now, but sometimes my heart still hurts a little when I think about that situation.

I thought this girl really loved me. I thought she really cared. But one day during lunchtime, in front of the whole cafeteria crowd, she broke up with me. I was so embarrassed and heartbroken. It took me a very long time to ever have a girlfriend again. That same pain carried into my teenage years and into my adulthood. It took years for me to get healed from that broken childhood relationship. In fact, that experience affected most of my youth. It caused me to believe I wasn't worthy of being loved.

Because I never dealt with those feelings, I carried that pain throughout high school and into adulthood. I got married at a young age, and that marriage ended in divorce. Even while I was married, it was hard for me to believe that someone could really love me, even if they told me so. After my marriage ended, I realized I needed to take time and allow God to heal me from that brokenness. Along the way I had many broken relationships. Now I'm in a place where I can encourage you to allow God to heal you.

What does this have to do with waiting? You must understand that the fact that you're strong doesn't mean you will heal easily. Broken relationships take time to get over. You can get over them, but you must let God heal you. Do not rush the process. Let God restore you. God can fix your broken relationships. He has an abundance of both love and patience. But you must understand that it's going to take time. As I said before, if you're trying to heal from a broken relationship or if you're trusting God to fix your broken relationships, you are going to have to respect the process.

One thing that you must refuse to do while you are trying to heal from a broken relationship is to go back to it. Do not return to the places God delivers you from. Some relationships are meant to break. Some relationships are purposeful in their ending. There are some doors God shuts in our lives to bless us.

Some relationships are burdens and not blessings. Every time you go back to something God wants you out of, you settle for less than what you deserve, less than what God wants for you. Don't lose self-respect because you get tired of waiting on God. If you rush back into relationships that are meant to be broken, you will rush into misery. God didn't create you to be miserable; He created you to be blessed. But know this: God can restore things that are broken and change them into things that are awesome. Perhaps God wants to fix your broken relationships. Whatever His plan is, you have to believe that your waiting season is not a waste. God is doing something great. He is either going to direct you away from that relationship or He's going to direct you to mend it.

Don't Rush

The Lord spoke to me one night. He said, "Marcus, when you rush into a relationship, you can rush into misery." When the Lord spoke that word to me, it shook me. At that time I desperately wanted to be in a romantic relationship. I was feeling lonely, and I got tired of waiting. I was watching others getting married, and I wanted to get married too. It was almost as if I was willing to settle for anyone just to be in a relationship. I didn't realize that the best relationship to have was a relationship with God. I didn't even understand the value in having a strong relationship with myself. I was in a rush to connect with another individual so I could say I was married. I wish that I knew then what I know now about waiting on God.

Waiting on God is a little painful at times, but it's actually the best place to be. You get to learn more about yourself. You get to draw closer to God. You get to be made stronger in areas where you are weak. God is so amazing, and we learn more about His amazing power while we wait on Him to fully manifest that power in our lives.

But instead of waiting, I rushed into a relationship and then into marriage. I did exactly what God said not to do, and it led to heartache. As God said to me, I say to you: when you rush into a relationship or marriage, you can rush into misery.

Some of the most miserable seasons of my life were when I had to endure the consequences of rushing into relationships. I'm using my testimony to encourage you. If you are waiting for a romantic relationship to manifest itself in your life, the worst thing you can do is rush into it. Please take your time. I beseech you to enjoy your waiting time. The longer you wait, I believe, the greater the blessing.

There are times when it's OK to be in a rush. When you are rushing, you're advancing rapidly. Sometimes rushing is necessary, but when it comes to building relationships with people, rushing shouldn't even be a consideration. You never want to make any sudden decisions when it comes to your heart. You never should be in such a hurry that you step out of God's perfect will for your life. As I mentioned earlier in this book, God's permissive will and God's perfect will are two totally different things. I learned a powerful lesson.

When I rushed into marriage, I ended up living in God's permissive will, and I found myself surviving instead of thriving. Take it from me, that's one place that you don't want to be. You'll end up praying for a way of escape from your situation. So, again I say, do not rush.

I know that you're excited about romance and there is a sense of urgency in your heart to be with somebody, but you cannot progress excessively. Rushing will cause you to miss out on three things.

1. You will miss out on opportunities.

When we rush into relationships, we end up distracted from the great opportunities that God has for us. You have an amazing career. You have a great vision for your life. You have an amazing future. When you move too quickly, you end up committing to something that can actually be a distraction from making your dreams come true. Don't miss out on wonderful opportunities or open doors because you choose to rush into a relationship. The relationship you rush into could be the wrong relationship. This is why you cannot afford to ignore God's voice.

2. You will miss the voice of God.

The voice of God is the main tool through which we receive guidance from the Lord. God really does speak to us. But if we're rushing to do things God is trying to warn us against, we will miss His voice. Don't rush and get distracted and end up not hearing God's voice clearly.

3. You will miss your real answer.

What if you rush into the wrong relationship with the wrong person, and the right person was being prepared for you? I rushed into many bad relationships, and I believe that's why I was so miserable for a season. You will only win if you choose to wait. Rushing leads to settling. You were not created to settle. Settling has everything to do with deciding to commit to less than what God wants for you.

Don't do it. Don't limit yourself. Don't allow yourself to be so broken and impatient that you rush into heartache. Don't be so quick. You may miss out on God's best for you. Swiftness is a good thing in some instances. But when it comes to waiting on God's best concerning your relationships, making a hasty commitment is a bad idea.

FAMILY RELATIONSHIPS

Let me begin this section by saying this: I believe God wants to bless your family beyond measure! He has a special miracle for your entire family, and in His perfect timing the release is going to take place. Family is so important. In fact, before there was a church, there was family. I've adopted this concept even in my personal life, that family always comes first. God has a special blessing for you and your family, but it will take time to see that blessing come to pass. Nothing happens overnight.

You may be close to God, but are all of your family members close to God? There is a burden we all carry when we know that we have family members who do not know God. Perhaps you've been waiting to see your spouse come to the Lord. Or maybe you've been praying for your children to get saved. The good news is that your prayers will be answered—in God's perfect timing. Declare that your family belongs to the kingdom of God (Acts 16:31), and trust that God will perfect that which concerns you as it relates to your family (Ps. 138:8). It is His desire that all would be saved and come into the knowledge of the truth (1 Tim. 2:4).

While you're waiting on God to bless your family, understand this: no family is perfect. No family in this world is flawless. If you look at the lineage of Jesus, you'll see that there was dysfunction even in Jesus's family line. The fact that your family is dysfunctional doesn't mean you have to be dysfunctional. Every family has something in its makeup that isn't good. Family members argue and fight. There are even times when family members stop talking to one another. But even after all of the arguing and fighting, family is still family.

You may be waiting for your family situation to change. I have been in that position. You can see that your family is not doing so well, and your prayer is that your family would prosper together. I've actually been excited about the fact that God is using me to help change my family's situation. God has used me to help change my whole family's perspective on life. And it's a blessing to see how many family members have been willing to follow me as I follow Christ. I have some good news for you. You can be the carrier of the blessing for your family. I believe you are the reason your family is getting ready to be blessed beyond measure—because you are willing to wait on God for His best.

Keep waiting with joy, and you will see your family change for the good. While you're waiting on God to change your family, never stop doing the little things for them. Don't stop telling them you love them. Don't stop communicating with them. Don't ever get so frustrated while you're waiting for God to change your family that you decide to give up on them and God. Don't use this waiting time to bash your family. Don't waste time in this season being upset about your family situation. Use this waiting time to pray for your family. Use the power in your mouth to decree and declare that your family is blessed beyond measure. Declare that generational curses are broken. Declare that you will not make the same mistakes that some of your ancestors made. Allow God to use you to lead your family into their promised land.

Sometimes you'll have a family member who purposely rebels against what could be good for the rest of the family. I don't know why this happens, but it does. I hate to say this, but it's so true: when you have a family member who doesn't want to cooperate with what God wants to do in your family, you have a right to disconnect from that person just as you have a right to disconnect from toxic people. Some people, unfortunately, will drain the life out of you. These are the family members whom you have to love from a distance while you wait for them to accept God's best for them.

Some say that the greatest institution on earth is the family. Family is of God. Peace is of God. When you have family and peace of mind working together, you can have a pleasurable life. Perhaps you're praying that your family will be restored. You may be a parent who doesn't have a good relationship with your children. If you're like me, you're tired of seeing so many divorces happening in the body of Christ.

Family counts. Wait for God to restore them. Do not try to change your family by yourself. Only God can do that, so let Him be God for your family. Trust in the Lord with all your heart. He's going to do it! I decree and declare that your family is blessed!

ROMANTIC RELATIONSHIPS

Not everyone in this world desires to be married, but a lot of people do. I believe that being in a romantic relationship is a wonderful thing, especially when it leads to a happy marriage. Marriage is one of God's greatest gifts to mankind after salvation. There are lots of people in the world who want to win in their romantic relationships, but one of the reasons romantic relationships fail is because people fail to wait for the right person. When you commit to a romantic relationship with the wrong person, you are guaranteed to have the wrong experience.

Why not use your waiting time preparing for the person God has for you instead of trying to change your relationship status in your own strength? I believe your romantic relationship status will change or improve when you focus on your relationship status with God.

Romance is simply the feeling of excitement that is associated with love. So when people are in romantic relationships, they are in relationships that make them excited about love. There's nothing wrong with wanting to be excited about love, but the best thing to do with your excitement is to prepare for your relationship to last for a lifetime. Don't allow your eagerness for a romantic relationship cause you to rush into a relationship with somebody who simply looks good on the outside. Love is about appreciating a person for who he or she is on the inside. It's easy to fall in love with somebody because of their good looks, but it takes time to fall in love with somebody because of who they are inside. God's timing is perfect as it concerns our romantic relationships. He doesn't want you to fall in love with a person's costume. The Bible gives us great advice in 1 John 4:1 when it says, "Beloved, do not believe every spirit, but test the spirits to see whether they are from God, because many false prophets have gone out into the world." Actors in a movie wear costumes and play certain roles just to entertain you. They don't normally behave in real life the way they do in the film. They usually don't even look like the characters they portray. This is the same thing that happens in many romantic relationships, and I believe this is why so many of them don't work. You get two people who don't want to wait on God's perfect timing for the relationship, and they fall in love with each other's costumes. Then the costumes come off and they see a person they never knew behind the mask.

It is unfortunate that many get married while ignoring the voice of God and speedily commit to the person's costume instead of taking time to find out who that person really is. There are so many who are hurting in relationships because they fell in love with the person's mask without taking time to find out if they could fall in love with the person's true character. Don't allow your excitement over what you see on the outside cause you to rush into a romantic relationship. You may find out the person was just wearing a costume, and what is underneath the costume could become your biggest burden. I've experienced this more than once myself, and I've learned the hard way that it's better to wait on God.

Your romantic relationship status will change when you focus on your relationship status with God.

Here's a big piece of advice, and I hope you'll be able to receive this. While you are waiting on God for your romantic relationship, be open to change. God may be preparing you to fall in love with the most unexpected person. God has an amazing way of doing that. He will bring someone into your life you never expected, and He will cause it to happen at the most unexpected time. I've seen this happen. God will connect you with somebody who will be everything you prayed for—and it will happen at just the right time.

Physical attraction is definitely important, but a real emotional and mental connection is even more significant. Trust God with your romantic relationships, and be patient while you wait for Him to bring the right person into your life. During that time, allow God to shape you. Allow Him to prepare your heart for the romance of your future.

I know you may feel lonely right now, or you may be worried that your current relationship is not going to work out. I want to encourage you with this fact: God's timing is flawless as it concerns your romantic experience. God loves you. The Lord will surely connect you with the right person who will love you the right way.

Business and Professional Relationships

One Sunday evening when I was returning to Winston-Salem, North Carolina, from New York, I was sitting in baggage claim waiting for the attendant to let me know whether my bag had arrived. I was frustrated because the baggage claim representative told me the airline made a mistake in New York and my luggage would be on the next flight into Greensboro, but that plane wasn't scheduled to land for another four hours. I decided to just wait at the airport. As frustrated as I was, I kept calm and tried to relax.

While I was sitting there, a gentleman approached me. He said, "Hey, young man, have you ever thought about owning your own business?" I said, "Of course. Why do you ask?" He proceeded to talk to me about a business he was a part of. Then he invited me to come and hear a presentation at an upcoming meeting. I was excited about going because I had never been to a professional business meeting before.

A few days later I went to the meeting. I was dressed

professionally in a suit. I sat in that business presentation and learned so much. I didn't join the business, but I walked away from that meeting with a brand-new perspective on how I could be successful. That man planted a seed in my life, and I have never been the same since.

This is why I say God's timing is perfect as it concerns our business relationships. I had seen the airline mishandling my luggage as an inconvenience. But my inconvenience ended up working for my good. If my luggage had not been misplaced, I would have left the airport and never would have met that nice gentleman. If I'd never met him, I wouldn't have sat through that business presentation. Without that experience I wouldn't have been motivated at that perfect time to be where I am now.

What I'm trying to say is that God's timing is perfect when it comes to meeting the people who will bless us professionally. My daily prayers include these words, and I would encourage you to include them in your prayers as well: "God, I thank You for placing the right people across my path. Let me be a blessing to them, and let them be a blessing to me."

When you pray prayers like this, you prepare yourself to meet people who will bless your career or business. Some of those people you will be connected to for a season, and others you will know for a lifetime. I've even found that some business relationships turn into genuine friendships. But it's best not to take matters into your own hands. You have to allow God to connect you with the right people.

As you wait on God to connect you with the right individuals, ask Him to prepare you so you will be ready when you do meet them. Your interviews will go so much better if you take time to prepare. Meetings over coffee or on the golf course will run more smoothly if you wait on God to make the connection. When the time comes for the meeting, God will give you the right words to say. God will even give you guidance on what to wear and how to properly prepare your presentations.

One connection can open incredible doors for you. I once heard a great preacher say, "Favor is about having the right person like you." Believe me when I tell you, I have met some awesome individuals in some high places. It was my personality, humility, and disposition that suggested I wasn't in a hurry that caused them to open doors for me.

When God places these connections in your life, you have to recognize them for who they are and for the assignment that God has them on. Always find a way to be a blessing to them first before you look for them to open doors and bless you.

I remember meeting a very famous actress. Of course, I wanted to take a photo with her, but before I took the photo, I asked her if I could pray and speak a blessing over her life. She really appreciated that, and she never forgot me. That connection opened more doors for my business and career. Why? I didn't take for granted the opportunity to connect with this individual. I saw it as a God moment. I whispered this prayer to the Lord: "Lord, don't let me miss this moment. If there's anything in this moment I need to see, lead me and guide me so that I make the best out of this." My prayers blessed her, and she was glad to take a photo with me that I was able to share with the world.

I declare that God is going to connect you with the right people and you will build the best business relationships.

Those individuals will benefit you, and you will benefit them. Your gift will make room for you. God will surround you with the right people who will teach you and prepare you for the next level. My old pastor in Fayetteville, North Carolina, told me these words before I went to college. He said, "Never be the smartest person in your circle." I held on to those words as if they would save my life. And they certainly did.

If you're the smartest person in your circle, you will never learn anything. You will always be pouring out, and that can be draining. But if you surround yourself with people who know more than you or have more experience than you do, you'll always be in position to learn more if those individuals are willing to share. The relationships God is going to give you as it concerns your business are going to be

Declare: I will not force relationships, but I will let God build divine relationships!

with people who are willing to share. The Bible says in Proverbs 11:14, "In the multitude of counselors there is safety." God's timing is perfect. He will connect you with professional and successful individuals who will be excited about helping you get to the next level!

SPIRITUAL RELATIONSHIPS

There is a difference between being religious and having a relationship with God. I don't consider myself a religious person. My goal is to have a true connection with the Father. On my spiritual journey I've learned that it is important to have people around me who are seeking the same thing. Life is so much easier when the people close to you also have a deep relationship with God. There have been times in my life when I've been confused and was able to call on someone who was spiritually mature enough to help me get through that confusion.

I've grown so much in the Lord because God has blessed me to be surrounded by people who can help me to grow closer to Him. The Bible says in Psalm 1:1, "Blessed is the man who walks not in the counsel of the ungodly, nor stands in the path of sinners, nor sits in the seat of scoffers." This verse gives us some of the best advice we can grab hold of during our waiting season: spend time with godly people, and you will be blessed. Plain and simple.

The Word of God also tells us in 2 Corinthians 6:14, "Do not be unequally yoked together with unbelievers. For what fellowship has righteousness with unrighteousness? What communion has light with darkness?" So many people waste time with the wrong people, and that's why they stay discouraged. While you wait for your miracle, you must have someone in your life you can depend on to pray for you and push you to the next level in God. A lot of people say that all they need is Jesus. We do need Jesus, but the Lord also will place people in our lives to help us grow closer to Him.

Here are five ways spiritually strong people will help you grow in your season of waiting.

1. Prayer

Having spiritual relationships will help you to pray more. Your personal prayer life will be developed when you pray with those who have a stronger prayer life. As you wait on God, it's important for you to spend time in prayer and learn to hear God's voice. I believe that God helps us hear His voice by connecting us with people who know how to hear Him clearly.

I learned how to hear the voice of the Lord from my grandfather. I noticed that during his prayer time he would speak to the Lord and then be silent. I asked him why he got silent in the middle of his prayers. He said, "Son, I'm listening to the voice of the Lord." If I did not have that type of spiritual relationship with my grandfather, I might have never learned many of the things I know today.

The Bible says in James 5:16, "Confess your faults to one another and pray for one another, that you may be healed. The effective, fervent prayer of a righteous man accomplishes much." My grandmother is a strong prayer warrior too. She would go to the church at 5:00 a.m. every weekday and pray before the Lord at the altar. She prayed alone for a few months. Then after a while I started going with her to the church to pray. This is where I developed my prayer life. The spiritual relationship I had with my grandmother motivated me to pray more. I also learned how to seek God and allow Him to fill me with His anointing.

As you are waiting on God to answer your prayers, connect with some spiritually mature individuals who can help you pray and hear from the Lord.

2. Knowledge of the Word

Spiritual relationships also help you grow more in the Word. The Bible says in Psalm 119:11, "Your word I have hidden in my heart, that I might not sin against You." Spiritual people are full of the Word of God, and they live the Word. Spiritual people are walking examples of what it means to be true children of God.

When you allow God to build your spiritual relationships with people like this, you begin to grow in the Word too. Spiritual people speak the Word. They don't speak their opinions. When you're surrounded by people who are always speaking their opinions, you grow in their opinions, and then you're inspired to live by your opinions as well. But when you surround yourself with spiritual people who speak the Word of God, you become inspired to speak and live by the Word of God. The Word of God is your foundation. You should be standing on it while you're waiting.

When I moved into my dorm in my freshman year of college, I put some inappropriate photos on my wall. I was a church boy, but I figured once I got to college, I was going to be loose and free. Well, my next-door neighbor was also a church boy, but he wasn't religious. He had a real relationship with God. When he saw the pictures on my wall, he quickly began to declare God's Word. I was so convicted that I took the pictures down. He and I were close friends all the way through college. He helped me stay close to the Lord. This is one of the benefits of having good spiritual relationships.

While you're waiting on God, connect with people who are close to the Lord and will help you through. Spend time with them. Hold conversations and Bible studies with those individuals who have good revelation of God's Word. Spiritual relationships will also increase your faith. When you're waiting on God, doubt can creep it. You need .to be around people who are going to give you a faith charge. You need to be around people who have had to use their faith to get through. Most spiritual people have a powerful testimony. They can tell you what it means to activate your faith and be healed. They can tell you what it means to believe God for financial miracles. They can tell you what it means to wait on God and believe that His best is being prepared for you. I love spending time with people of faith.

3. Faith

I remember speaking with a pastor about how he was able to believe God for a miracle his ministry had recently experienced. Spending time with this spiritual man did nothing but stir my faith even more. I walked away from that conversation with no doubt in my mind that God was getting ready to do something great in my life. This pastor already had the answer to his prayers. I was waiting on my answer. Being around this man of God gave me the faith charge I needed to continue to wait expectantly for what God was going to do in my life. In your waiting season, I encourage you to get around some people who will charge and build your faith.

4. Patience

Another benefit of having spiritual relationships is that you learn patience. You will not learn how to properly wait on God if you're in relationships with people who are always in a rush. The Bible tells us to wait patiently for the Lord (Ps. 37:7). Patience is a virtue. Spiritual people are patient people. They trust God. They know how to properly wait on the Lord. Even when things look bad, they still trust in God's perfect timing. Spiritual relationships will develop your patience. The right people will encourage you and remind you to hold on just a little while longer because everything is going to be all right.

You need to build spiritual relationships that will push you and help you understand that great things come out of patience. Patience isn't just having the ability to wait; it's about how you act while you wait. Are you at peace or frustrated while you wait? Are you standing in faith or doubting every moment while you wait? Are you surrendering to God or trying to make things happen in your own strength? The right people in your life will help you wait the right way.

5. Love

Spiritually strong people are full of the love of God. The Bible says in 1 John 4:7–8, "Beloved, let us love one another, for love is of God, and everyone who loves is born of God and knows God. Anyone who does not love does not know God, for God is love." One of the best ways to discern whether someone is truly walking with God is to observe how they share God's love.

Having a relationship with someone who is close to God will help you learn how to love better too. You have to love your journey. You have to love your season. You have to love yourself. And even though you don't understand how and why God may be doing certain things in your life, you can't stop loving God. As a child of God, you may find it easy to love the Lord. Just thinking about His goodness and all He has done for you probably causes love and gratitude to well up in your heart. But spiritual relationships will help you to love your enemies too. They will help you to forgive those who have hurt you.

Having the right people in your life will push you in the right direction of pleasing God for the rest of your life. These are the people who may not always tell you what you want to hear, but what they share will always be what you need to hear. Their ability to hold you accountable to God is a great sign that they really love you. A person who is in your life on assignment from God will share with you things you need to know to save your life. Be willing to receive them in your life and know that they are there to bless you and not to harm you.

Who you are connected to is important to God. Trust Him with your relationships. He knows what is best.

PRAY!

Father, I thank You for blessing me with good relationships. I pray that every bad relationship in my life would be dismissed. I ask You, Lord, to connect me with the right people, people who will push me to the next level, in Jesus's name, amen.

NOW, DECLARE!

- God is placing the right people in my life who will push me to the next level; as I walk with the wise, I will become wise (Prov. 13:20).

- Bad company corrupts good character; therefore I will not be distracted by the wrong relationships (1 Cor. 15:33).

- Because iron sharpens iron, I will recognize and respond when God connects me with people of wisdom (Prov. 27:17).

- Just as God brought Elijah into Elisha's life to take Elisha to the next level, God is placing people in my life who will bless me and not burden me (1 Kings 19:16, 19). I will not force relationships, but I will let God build divine relationships.

- The most important relationship I will ever have is with God; as I am drawing near to God, He is drawing near to me (James 4:8).

Chapter 8

GOD'S TIMING FOR RELEASING HIS FAVOR

SOME TIME AGO I created a post on Facebook in which I used the photo of a large city skyline. I wanted to create an image of a prosperous lifestyle. I also used it to express a declaration the Lord had given me to encourage people. The meme read, "God will give you a job that pays more than you ever imagined, and you're not even educationally qualified for it. That's called favor." It seemed to be just what people needed to hear, because it went viral.

At the time I shared that message, I had about three thousand followers on Facebook. I was impressed with that number, but I had no idea what was getting ready to happen. The post reached millions of people and caused my social media platform to blast off!

In the post I was talking about how you don't have to work so hard to be blessed. This got people excited because I helped them see that God's favor is one of the greatest gifts He can give. With His favor God can blow our minds in an instant.

When the favor of God is on your life, the unthinkable happens. When the favor of God is on your life, dreams come true. When the favor of God is on your life, you are rewarded without having to work so hard.

I'm sure thousands of the people who read that post had been praying for an increase or promotion on their jobs. When they saw that post, it stirred their spirits. They realized that it's not always their degree or their educational background that will open doors for them to be blessed; sometimes it's God's favor.

The favor of God causes doors to be opened that we don't even deserve. While everybody else in the world is working so hard to gain, we work hard in the spirit. God recognizes our love for Him and finds ways to bless us.

A lot of people think it's wrong to survive off God's favor. I think it's the best way to live. God's favor is multiplied on us every day. While you are in your waiting season, believe that His favor is on you now. Start declaring this: "I wake up with God's favor every single day." It's God's favor that allows you to survive throughout the day. It's the favor of God that allows you to wake up in the morning. It's the favor of God that allows you to have food to eat and clothes to wear. These examples may sound simple to you, but there are so many reasons we should rejoice over God's favor being with us daily. Favor is not something we should boast about. It is a gift from God, and we should forever be grateful for it.

Declaring that the favor of God is on your life is a part of our spiritual warfare. What if there are some things in your life that have not been released because you have not recognized that the favor of God is on you? What if the Lord is waiting for you to recognize that His favor is the key to your blessings? When God's favor is on your life, the devil and his demons cannot suppress your miracle. God's favor on your life causes release to happen. When His favor is on your life and you recognize it and live by it, miracles take place sooner than you expected.

Knowing that God's favor will cause a release to happen quickly is more than enough reason to praise God in advance!

Jesus said, "I came that they may have life, and that they may have it more abundantly" (John 10:10). That means we have the favor of God on our lives. This favor causes the ground to shake when you need to be freed from your present situation. This favor causes the Red Sea to split open so you can walk on dry ground from your place of misery to your place of freedom.

> When the favor of God is on your life, the unthinkable happens. When the favor of God is on your life, dreams come true. When the favor of God is on your life, you are rewarded without having to working so hard.

Creating that Facebook post sent a mighty wave through social media. I believe that because of it thousands of people were convinced that with the favor of God, everything they touched would prosper from that moment forward. Sometimes all it takes for the favor of God to be released in a mighty way is for a man or woman of God to send a prophetic word into the atmosphere.

God can and will use you to do the same—to speak His favor over your household, your job situation, your ministry. Speak and declare that the favor of God is hovering over anything concerning you. Stir up your faith to declare, "No matter what, I'm living with the favor of God." You will begin to see quick results in your life—results that agree with God. You will confuse the enemy. He will be left to wonder how you are being so blessed. Your answer will immediately be, "I'm one of God's favorites, and His favor is on my life right now!"

WHAT IS FAVOR ANYWAY?

To truly appreciate God's amazing gift of favor, which is one of the greatest blessings mankind could have, we need to understand what it is. Knowing what favor is will get you more excited about having it, and you'll gain a true sense of why God chooses to give it to you. So let's take some time to break down the meaning of this powerful gift called favor.

To have favor simply means that you are in a position of receiving approval. When someone takes a liking to something, it means the person favors that thing. And when they favor something, they tend to perform acts of kindness that go beyond what is usual. We all receive a certain level of favor, but the favor I am talking about is when you receive kindness, love, or goodness that goes beyond the norm. It's about getting rewarded for more than what you actually earned. That's favor! Favor is a sign of approval. It's fortunate goodwill. I like to say that favor is exaggerated kindness.

When someone shows approval of your preference or of

who you are, you can declare that you have favor with that person. When you recognize that you or something you've accomplished is being honored, that is a sign that you're being shown favor.

Psalm 5:12 says, "For You, LORD, will bless the righteous; You surround him with favor like a shield." God's favor rests on the righteous, those who have chosen to live in obedience to Him. When the favor of God is on your life, it's safe to say that God is satisfied with you. When God is satisfied with you, you know for certain that the windows of heaven are going to be open for you.

> Declare this right now: I'm one of God's favorites, and His favor is on my life!

God will begin to pour out blessings over your life that you won't have room to receive. Why am I so confident about this? Because this is what happens when God delights in His child.

Having the favor of God suggests that God is willing to make accommodations for you that exceed what you might have asked for or imagined. What an amazing position to be in, where you have such a relationship with God that He is willing to bless you extravagantly, to pour into your life things that He knows you need or just desire to have. I believe the Bible when it says that God takes pleasure in the prosperity of His servants (Ps. 35:27, KJV). He pours out His favor on His children because He approves of them.

Some people have a hard time believing that God approves of them, but the Bible tells us so in Romans 4.

> What can we say that we have discovered about our ancestor Abraham? If Abraham had God's approval because of something he did, he would have had a reason to brag. But he could not brag to God about it. What does Scripture say? "Abraham believed God, and that faith was regarded as the basis of Abraham's approval by God." When people work, their pay is not regarded as a gift but something they have earned. However, when people don't work but believe God, the one who approves ungodly people, their faith is regarded as the basis of God's approval.
> —ROMANS 4:1–5, GW

Instead of using the words "God's approval," other translations say our faith in Christ is "credited as righteousness" (MEV; see also the KJV and NIV). If you have accepted Christ as your Savior and have chosen to follow Him, you are righteous in Christ, and that means you have God's approval. I want you to get that down in your spirit. God approves of you! You are His favorite, because favor is evidence that you have been approved by God.

To have the favor of God is to be blessed beyond measure. The Bible tells us that Isaac had God's favor, and even though he sowed seed during a drought, he still reaped a hundredfold (Gen. 26:1, 12). He was walking in the favor of God.

We can do the same. Isaiah 66:2 says, "These are the ones I look on with favor: those who are humble and contrite in spirit, and who tremble at my word" (NIV). God shows favor to those who delight in Him and seek Him above all else. It is His great desire to show us favor. Second Chronicles 16:9 says, "For the eyes of the LORD run to and fro throughout the whole earth, to shew himself strong in the behalf of them whose heart is perfect toward [completely committed to] him" (KJV).

When you have the favor of God, He will go above and beyond to provide for you. To be one of God's favorites simply means that God has favorable and friendly feelings toward you. God has truly taken you into consideration. The favor of God opens the door for God to take careful thought of how He wants to work a miracle in your life. He does this because He is our friend (John 15:15) and He is our help (Ps. 54:4).

This is why you cannot get impatient during this waiting time. When you know that the favor of God is on your life, you know that God is simply taking time to prepare His best for you. You must believe God despite what you see in the natural. You must know that God has not forgotten about you.

How Favor Works With Compassion

God's favor and His compassion toward you are closely connected. To be compassionate simply means that one has concern for the sufferings or misfortunes of others. Do you not know that God is truly concerned about you? The Bible tells us in 1 Peter 5:7 to cast our cares upon Him because He cares for us. And Isaiah 30:18 says, "The LORD longs to be gracious to you; therefore he will rise up to show you compassion" (NIV).

Because God is concerned about you, He will not allow you to suffer forever. It is God's favor that rescues us from our suffering. Favor doesn't always manifest as a material blessing, but God's favor can always been seen in the fact that He is concerned about our victory. When God does whatever He needs to do to make sure that you and I are not defeated, that is proof that His favor is truly on our lives. Once again it goes back to where we started. The favor of God is God's acts of kindness beyond what we deserve.

Let me ask you this question. Have you ever received something that you knew you didn't deserve? Has there ever been a time in your life when you knew you should have been punished for a thing, but you didn't get punished at all? Have you ever had a moment when a person in authority could have fired you, but you kept your job and soon after received a promotion? If you're like me, you've been through those things. Those are the times when we recognize that God's favor is truly on our lives. The favor of God is something you never want to lose. It is something that you want to keep and recognize for the rest of your life.

FINANCIAL FAVOR

I'm getting ready to declare a word that I know you will get excited about. Every time I declare this word at a live worship experience or even in a Facebook post, people rejoice at a level that you probably can't imagine. This is the word God is leading me to declare: financial miracles are real!

So many people miss out on financial miracles simply because they do not believe that financial blessings are real. What a sad place to be in. To never be able to experience the favor of God on your finances would certainly take a chunk out of your good life experience.

Most of the prayer requests I receive have everything to do with the need for a financial miracle. If you're waiting on a financial miracle, I have good news for you: there is such a thing as God's favor for your finances. All you have to do is truly open your heart to be able to receive God's wisdom and favor, and everything concerning your finances will be changed for the better. Not only will you begin to see a change in your finances, but you will also begin to see a change in your level of responsibility for your finances.

Financial responsibility releases God's favor on your finances.

There is a bittersweet idea to this whole experience of having God's favor on your finances. God will not release financial overflow until He sees that you are responsible with what you have now. You see, if God gave you a financial miracle and He knows you're not a good steward over what you have now, the financial miracle you received would not last long. This is why we have to properly prepare ourselves and be responsible over our money. Why get a financial miracle and not even have the opportunity to benefit from it because you're irresponsible? The favor of God doesn't work like that. Faith without works is dead. Being responsible with your miracle is part of working your faith.

At this point you're probably saying, "I'm ready for my financial blessing. I'm ready for the favor of God to be on my money!" Keep on decreeing and declaring that the favor of God is working for your finances, but don't stop working your gifts, and don't stop praying and believing God for the best.

Financial generosity releases God's favor on your finances.

One of the best ways to receive the favor of God on our finances is to be a giver. Generosity is one of the best ways to please God. This is the principle of sowing and reaping. Financial miracles happen when we sow seeds of faith into good ground expecting a great harvest in return. The blessings of Abraham belong to you. You must position yourself to receive a financial miracle by sowing the finances you have into good ground.

I remember the first time I sowed in a worship service. The man of God stood before the congregation and said, "I need faith believers to sow a one-hundred-dollar seed into the service." At that time a one-hundred-dollar offering was a big stretch for me, but because I was believing for the favor of God to be on my finances, I gave the one hundred dollars by faith. I believed that if I sowed into good ground, a big harvest would come my way in return. I can testify that a mighty harvest did come my way.

The Bible says, "Give, and it will be given to you: Good measure, pressed down, shaken together, and running over will men give unto you. For with the measure you use, it will be measured unto you" (Luke 6:38).

I have met so many people who say, "Pastor Marcus, I'm believing God for a financial blessing." They gave gifts of love through their finances into my ministry, and within hours, they have testified of receiving promotions, increase, and unexpected checks! This is certainly proof that God will work a miracle in your finances when you follow His leading to give.

Maybe you're reading this book and you are believing God for a financial miracle. I invite you to sow into good ground. Don't allow your seed to die in your hand. Release that seed of faith to the work of the Lord, and I promise you God will open the windows of heaven and shower down financial miracles on your life. Remember this: giving is not losing; giving is gaining. And in God's perfect timing, when He is ready to release that financial miracle into your hands, that financial blessing is going to come into your life.

There is perfect timing for the release of your financial miracle. You can't stop giving and thanking God in advance because the financial miracle hasn't come according to your timing. Do you want a tainted financial blessing? I hope you want a perfected financial miracle. It is a great blessing when God finally releases the financial overflow in your life at the right time.

There was a season in my life when I desperately needed a financial turnaround. During that waiting season I felt like giving up on waiting on God and doing whatever I needed to do to get that need met. But I didn't. I turned to God and learned how to wait on Him. I kept serving, giving, and blessing others. I did all of that because I trusted God and believed that His perfect timing for financial favor and increase would be released when God said so.

Don't try to force the financial miracle to happen on your own. You will destroy your opportunity to receive a perfect blessing. You could possibly block your financial favor by attempting to do God's job. God can open financial doors for you that you would never imagine. I've seen it happen when the favor of God is resting on a person's finances. God's timing is always perfect, including when it comes to our money.

DO I DESERVE THIS?

Most of us work hard to receive a reward. We are told that nothing comes our way for free. As a young man growing up, I was reminded of 2 Thessalonians 3:10, which teaches that if you do not work, you do not eat. That verse was quoted to me many times to motivate me to get up, get out, and do something. If you don't get a job, you won't be able to receive the reward that would put you in position to enjoy life. Rewards don't come for nothing; you have to do something.

The question "Do I deserve this?" comes when we feel we haven't done enough to receive a great reward. Every day people go to work and earn a paycheck based on how much work they have done, the experience they have to do that job, and their level of education. But there are some times when a person might get a bonus. That bonus comes because your boss or company owner decides you should earn more because of the results you helped produce for the business.

Sometimes a bonus comes by surprise. When I was working at the Super 8 Motel, bonuses would come unexpectedly. I would ask my boss, "Did I earn this?" The boss would quickly say, "Yes, you did." I would then have to reflect on how much work I did. I know that I only did my job, but there was something about my work ethic that week that helped the hotel make more money. Even though I didn't recognize that my work ethic was benefiting the company, I still got paid more money than I expected.

This happened because the one in charge felt as if I deserved an increase. It was my faithfulness to the job, my nice smile to customers, and my ability to represent the company at such a high level of excellence that made the difference. My work in these areas contributed to the company's overall income, and my boss showed his approval by increasing my paycheck. Even when I didn't think I deserved the increase, my boss knew that I did.

Sometimes we have a similar experience with God, but with Him it's all part of His favor on our lives. When you get what you don't deserve, that's favor.

While you are waiting on God to answer your prayers, one of the best ways to avoid discouragement is to remember that it doesn't matter whether you feel you deserve to be blessed. It doesn't matter whether you feel you deserve to prosper. You have God's favor. That means you have a reason to smile and rejoice, because God wants to bless you whether you think you deserve it or not. Yet the blessing will come in His time.

Sometimes waiting can be harder than we ever thought. You may wonder why you're having to wait so long, why you're having to endure this season when it seems God has forgotten about you. I want to give you this good news, and I hope you rejoice in it: this season of waiting is preparing you for the big blessing that is coming your way! God wants to bless you. He wants you to have good, healthy relationships. He wants you to prosper in your career. He wants your body to be healed. After all you've gone through, He wants you to come out with a blessing.

You are waiting because God is preparing this blessing for you. During your season of waiting you are building up qualities that are preparing you to handle the blessings God is going to pour on you. God has great things in store for you, and you are becoming a great person who can handle those blessings. Never settle for less than what God desires for you. When you settle for less, you miss out on receiving God's best. Never allow yourself to be so impatient or desperate for an answer to prayer or a blessing that you end up settling for a much smaller blessing than the big blessing God was preparing for you.

If you're thinking, "Pastor Marcus, I really feel as if my life should be better," then that, perhaps, is a sign that it should. The great things that God has in store for you are only going to come when you recognize that you are good enough for them. Don't allow the negative elements of your life to convince you that you don't deserve God's best.

You deserve honesty, transparency, respect, love, and appreciation in life. It's times like what you may be going through now that help you realize you deserve better than what you've been settling for in life. This realization makes it easier for you to walk away from the places, people, and things you know God didn't prepare for you. You may have to walk away from that relationship. You may have to walk away from that church you've attended for years.

No matter what, do not let the enemy convince you that you don't deserve God's best. You deserve exactly what God desires for you—His absolute best—and it is being prepared for you right now.

GOD'S GOODNESS

God is good. First Peter 5:10 gives us a great description of God's goodness when it says, "But after you have suffered a little while, the God of all grace, who has called us to His eternal glory through Christ Jesus, will restore, support, strengthen, and establish you." How could we talk about God's favor without talking about God's goodness? It would be impossible. It is the goodness of the Lord that allows us to obtain His favor. I believe that God's favor is the harvest that comes from God's goodness. Something that is good is generally desired or approved of. Though God doesn't need our approval, any person in their right mind would desire God.

The personality and character of God is the highest-ranking character there is. God's status is so high, there is nothing that compares to His level of quality. When I think of God and His goodness, I think of the perfection of God Himself. Out of His perfection flows excellence, benevolence, virtue, charity, goodwill, kindness, mercy, and peace. The Lord is our source of all of these things, and He is the greatest example of them. God is simply our superior, and when our superior shares His goodness with us, we can't help but show evidence of favor!

There's one thing I know: God has been good to me. I'm reminded of what David said in Psalm 23:6, "Surely goodness and mercy shall follow me all the days of my life." Look at that word *goodness*. What is David talking about when he says goodness? I believe that David was talking about the goodness of the Lord. In fact, to be more specific for the purpose of motivating you, I believe David was rejoicing in the fact that he knew that God's goodness, or His favor, would follow him all the days of his life. When he used the word *follow*, he meant that he would carry those attributes with him wherever he went every day until he died.

All the days of our life are not going to be full of answers. You may have some days when you have to wait on God. You may have some days when you don't see the answer to your prayers fully manifested in your life. But surely the favor of God, His goodness and mercy, is with you every day of your life. If you're waiting on God to do something miraculous in your life right now, then know this: the goodness of the Lord is with you even while you wait. It will never leave you. You have to believe this with all of your heart.

Sometimes in the waiting season it feels as if the goodness of the Lord is not with you, but you have to declare, "Surely the goodness of the Lord is following me. Surely the goodness of the Lord is with me." The qualities and standards of excellence that make God who He is are on your life right now. The Bible says, "Taste and see that the LORD is good" (Ps. 34:8). Give that a try. You may say, "I've been waiting and waiting and waiting." But you have to declare that God is still good. How we think about God determines how we respond to God. I've met so many people who don't respond to God in a good way because they don't think of God in a good way. Some think that because they are waiting on God to answer their prayers, He is a bad God.

When people think of God as a bad God, they respond to Him in a bad way. Don't let that be your testimony.

Think of God and His goodness even when things don't go your way. When you think of God in a good way, you will respond to God in a good way. When you think of God and His goodness, your response to God will be one of goodness. How you respond to God is very important in this season. Respond to God with goodness, kindness, love, gentleness, and long-suffering! You could never find yourself getting fed up with God. When you get tired of God, you get tired of His goodness.

One of the things that I have discovered in life is that when you expect greatness, you experience greatness. Thinking about the goodness of God will take your faith to a greater level. For example, if you are believing God for a friend to receive Christ as their personal Savior, thinking of how God saved you or another friend will give you the faith charge you need to expect Him to do it again. If you're waiting on God to do something big in your life, build your faith by reflecting on His goodness to you in the past so you can easily expect Him to work a miracle again. When David was preparing to face Goliath, His faith was charged as he anticipated the victory. He was not afraid, and he didn't doubt because his view of God was good. David was able to reflect on how God delivered Him from previous battles against a lion and a bear, and that gave him the confidence to know that God would deliver him again (1 Sam. 17:33–37).

God's goodness is working for you even when you cannot see it, so don't ever despise the goodness of the Lord. You have to remain confident that you will see the goodness of the Lord in the land of the living, as Psalm 27:13 says. Once you've had the opportunity to feast on the goodness of the Lord, nothing in this world will be more satisfying.

During this waiting time commit yourself to keeping your mind on the goodness of God. Think about the great things God has already done in your life. David had confidence while he was waiting to win another battle because he was able to reflect on the goodness of the Lord. And because of the favor of God, David gained the victory over his enemy. You and I have that same favor on our lives today. But that favor is because of God's goodness. When you reflect on the overwhelming goodness of God, you will not be able to help but rejoice. It's all a part of His favor. God is a good God!

SEEKING GOD'S FAVOR

Perhaps you really don't know if the favor of God is on your life. You may say, "I believe it's there, but I want to see the manifestation of it." That is a good thing. We all want to recognize the favor of God on our lives. Sometimes we have to be pushed into seeing our situation the right way. There may be some things in our lives that we think are the favor of God but aren't the favor of God at all.

My grandfather taught me something a few years ago. He said that every good thing that comes your way isn't always from God, because the devil knows how to pass out blessings too! This was hard for me to understand at first, but after a while I got it. I realized that sometimes we seek good things, but what looks good to us is not always good for us. This is why it's important to know how to properly seek God's favor. You don't want to go through this waiting season and then accept something that is not really your blessing.

Why go through all this just to end up with the wrong answer? I've been there before. It takes us back to trying to survive in God's permissive will when God wants us to live in His perfect will. One who seeks is one who is attempting to find something. If you're seeking the favor of God, you desire to obtain it. So let's talk about some ways to know that God's favor is on your life.

1. Ask for it.

Don't be afraid to ask God for His favor. Even though we believe that God's favor is following us through life, we still must have enough faith to ask for it. Make your request known to God. Let God know that you need His favor. Of course, when you make a request, you are actively and formally *asking* for something. Don't ever command God. I really believe it's disrespectful when people demand that God do things. As you're seeking, make an appeal to the Lord, not a demand.

2. Be humble.

As you are seeking God's favor, walk with humility, knowing that it is God who gives the favor. It is not something we can work up ourselves.

3. Fast, pray, and read God's Word.

Your personal devotion time will draw you closer and closer to your opportunity to receive favor in its fullness. If you never pray, never read your Bible, and never fast, you will not put yourself in the position to receive what you have been seeking.

4. Put your faith into action.

Show God that you are hungry for more and that there's nothing in the world more important to you than obtaining what He has for you. The Bible says to ask, seek, and knock (Matt. 7:7–12). Your answer is not just going to fall from the sky. You must demonstrate your faith.

5. Connect with people who have favor.

Pay close attention to the people God places in your life. While you're seeking God's favor, God will connect you with people who have His favor on their lives. I have been through seasons in my life when I didn't know anybody who was happy. In some cases it was obvious that the favor of God was following certain people, but because they never tapped into that favor, they weren't enjoying the abundant life that Jesus promised us.

As I began to seek the favor of God, He began to connect me with people who live with His favor and are truly happy. I can testify that God will place the right people in your life, people who will bless you and be blessed by you. Don't get comfortable being around people who are not experiencing the authentic manifested power of God in their lives. You can encourage them, but don't spend all your life with them. They will hold you back. They will block you from receiving what God has for you.

God will place people in your life who will help you seek Him more—people who are hungry for more of God.

6. Seek the kingdom of God.

Jesus told us to seek first the kingdom of God and His righteousness, and all these things, including His favor, will be added to our life! (See Matthew 6:33.) This is the principal step to obtaining God's favor and recognizing when it is on your life. Don't seek the favor first; seek God first. This is the biggest piece of the puzzle.

Yes, God will connect you with God-seeking people. Yes, God will give you an opportunity to pray and ask for His favor. However, none of the steps will mean anything if you don't seek first the kingdom of God and His righteousness. In other words, you have to seek to know who God is, to know His character and how He works. The favor of God is on your life, but it's very important that you develop your personal relationship with God so you will be able to properly recognize when you're walking in His favor and when you're walking in your flesh.

Now notice what Jesus says in the second part of Matthew 6:33: after you seek first the kingdom of God and His righteousness, all the blessings will be added to you. Here comes the favor of God. Seeking God will end your search for favor. It will automatically be added to your life.

A wise man or woman will always put God first. Too often we spend our time searching for answers when what we really need to do is redirect our focus and search for God. When you seek God, you automatically obtain everything you need.

NEVER DOUBT

There was a time when I didn't know if God's healing power could flow through my ministry. I didn't discover that this anointing was real until a church member asked me to come to the hospital and pray for her dying daughter. I'll never forget it. I was about twenty-five years old. I got the phone call, and the church member said, "Minister Gill, the doctor said that my daughter will not live through the night. Can you come and pray?"

I was so nervous. I wondered how I could go and pray for someone if I wasn't sure God would heal that person. "What if she doesn't make it?" I thought. "How will they view God if she isn't healed?" I had so many questions in my head. The Lord quickly reminded me that His timing is always perfect.

My faith began to rise, and I thought that if God called me to preach and pray for people, then the anointing would be there and His perfect will would be done. At that moment I knew that it was the appointed time and God had put me on assignment to pray, and whether or not I had unshakable faith for this young lady to be healed, I had to say yes to the Lord.

When I arrived at the hospital, I was escorted to her room. I looked at the precious young lady, and she began to smile. I held her hand, laid hands on her forehead, and began to pray a prayer of healing. That night she not only accepted Christ as her personal Savior, but she also lived longer than the doctors said she would. She lived eight more months after the night I prayed for her.

God's timing is truly perfect. I have much respect for medical doctors, but they had set the wrong time for her to transition from this life to the next. They had determined that she would not survive the night. Even the family was convinced of the doctor's words. But God said otherwise. God's timing for her healing was totally different from the timing the doctors declared.

God's timing is more important than our timing. Even though she still ended up transitioning from this life to a heavenly life, there was reason to rejoice. As a result of her extended life, the young lady was able to experience three levels of healing: 1) The Lord gave her the blessed opportunity to accept Jesus Christ as her personal Savior; 2) her physical body was healed, and she was able to live and not die as they predicted; and 3) a few months later when she passed away, she got the ultimate healing. No more suffering. No more pain. She is now home with the Lord. The truth of the matter is that we all will go home to be with the Lord one day. But while we are here on the earth, God has a perfect time to release exactly what we need.

While you are in this season, you have the opportunity to increase your faith in the power, goodness, and favor of God. God wants to bless you. He wants you to walk in His favor. I dare you to put on your faith right now and declare that you will walk in the favor of God. Speak it aloud with boldness.

Whatever you are seeking God for, know that your faith and confidence in Him pleases Him. Do not doubt. Seek Him faithfully, for He is a rewarder of those who diligently seek Him (Heb. 11:6). If you have faith and do not doubt, the mountain you need moved will move (Matt. 21:21).

PRAY!

Lord, I thank You that Your unlimited goodness is chasing me down. I pray that a cloud of favor would hover over my head and rain blessings on my life like never before. I receive Your favor, in Jesus's name, amen.

Now, Declare!

- The blessing and favor of the Lord are on my life right now (Ps. 5:12).

- I choose to connect to people who have favor on their lives (Gen. 30:27).

- God is opening doors in my life that no man can shut (Isa. 22:22).

- Unexpected promotions and increase are searching for me (Deut. 28:2; see also Deuteronomy 28).

- I am the righteousness of God in Christ, and overflow comes to every area of my life (2 Cor. 5:21; 9:8).

Chapter 9

GOD'S TIMING FOR YOUR HEALING

OFTENTIMES A PERSON'S waiting season is also a person's healing season. Instead of focusing on receiving an answered prayer during this season, what if you took time to focus on getting healthy again? Yes, that includes physical, emotional, and spiritual health.

While you are waiting on God, it is very important that you recognize the areas in your life where you need to be healed. Healing is not just limited to physical healing. Healing doesn't only take place when a person is sick and wants to get better. Healing can also take place in your mind. Healing can take place in your emotions. Most people are not enjoying life because they are not healed spiritually. We all have been hurt at some point in time. We all have gone through seasons of life that were full of disappointments. The healing power of God is what helps us come from that place of disappointment to a new place of happiness and joy. Let the healing begin.

Jeremiah prayed for deliverance, saying, "Heal me, O Lord, and I will be healed; save me, and I will be saved, for You are my praise" (Jer. 17:14). When we are healed, it's as if God is alleviating anything in our lives that is causing us pain. While you are waiting to win, you must focus on recovering. When you recover from something, it means that you return to a normal state. One who is sick has to recover from that sickness and return to a state of health.

You may have been through some bad experiences and you're still holding on to the pain of those experiences. You need to return to a healthy state of mind. You need to recover. Perhaps the circumstances and burdens of life have taken your strength. You're probably reading this book right now and saying, "I need my strength back." I declare that healing is taking place and God is helping you to recover your strength.

This waiting season should be a season where you begin to regain possession of your faith. The Word of God is serving as your treatment. God is willing to provide you with everything you need to be healed. But you can't make God heal you the way you want to be healed. You have to allow God to heal you the way He wants to heal you. You must trust God and His process. The healing may not happen as quickly as you would like it to, but you have to believe that God's process is the best one for your life.

I've never been sick with a serious illness in my physical body, but I have been sick emotionally. After the death of my only child I went through an emotional sickness that almost led me to suicide. I would leave work every morning and try to figure out how I could kill myself without missing heaven. It wasn't until after I got divorced and began to get wise counsel that I realized how mentally sick I actually was. The fact that I was even thinking about suicide means I needed to seek real help.

There are a lot of people who are emotionally sick and don't even know it. I didn't know that I was coming to my end. I didn't realize that I was allowing my painful experience to cause me to nearly lose my mind. It wasn't until I got around people who were able to help me become spiritually and emotionally healthy that I realized God loved me and wanted to heal me.

When I discovered that, I wanted healing to take place in a split second, but I had to learn to wait for God's timing. It took

> The waiting season is the healing season.

Him a little while, but my healing came. And the only reason it came was because I cooperated with God and allowed Him to heal me.

The Bible says in James 5:15, "And the prayer of faith will save the sick, and the Lord will raise him up." Will you allow God to heal your heart? Will you make a conscious decision to desire healing so much that you lose yourself to God's will and His plan for your life and allow Him to do the healing in His way and in His timing? It takes courage to be healed, but I believe you have all the courage you need. When you are healed, it's proof that the pain no longer has control over you. It doesn't mean the pain never existed; it just means that you've made a decision to not allow the pain to rule your life.

One of the best ways to recognize that you've been healed—whether it's physical, spiritual, or emotional healing—is when you no longer feel pain from the thing that was hurting you. You have to imagine yourself dancing in the midst of the rain. You have to remember the times when storms came into your life to destroy you and God caused you to recover from those storms. Celebrate your victories, knowing that He will do the same for you again.

Your waiting season is a healing season. The Bible tells us in the Book of Isaiah that by His stripes we are healed (Isa. 53:5). You don't have to look for your healing. The Bible tells us that our healing has already happened. It's already done. Your opportunity to be healed is far greater than anyone's ability to hurt you. Make sure you stay connected to others who have been healed and who believe in and minister healing, and don't ever forget that God is the ultimate source for your healing.

If you begin to change the way you look at situations, your circumstances won't have the power to hold you in bondage. You have to see yourself healed. You have to speak of yourself as if you are free from sickness of any kind. To be healed is to recover. I declare that you are recovering while you wait so that when you get the blessing of winning, you won't be carrying the burden of losing.

HEALING AND THE PRESENCE OF GOD

Something awesome happens in the presence of God. Mighty things take place when we are in God's presence. When I have seen people physically healed, it always happened in the presence of the Lord. Notice that I didn't say it happened in church but rather in the presence of God. One place that you need to be while you're waiting for God's best for you is in His presence. You can invite the presence of God anywhere in your life. You don't necessarily have to wait until you get to church. You can feel God's presence in your house. His presence can be with you in your car on your way to work. His presence can be with you in the grocery store. His presence could be with you even if you happened to be in the hospital for a doctor's visit. It doesn't matter where you are; God's presence is available to you. It is in God's presence that we receive our healing.

Right now, while you're reading this book, the presence of God is with you. The presence of God is on me as I am writing this word to inspire you. Healing is taking place right now as these words of wisdom, inspired by God, are being downloaded into your spirit. Do as the Word says in 1 Samuel 12:16, "Even now, take your stand and see this great thing which the LORD is doing before your eyes."

Have you ever been in worship or in prayer and you felt the presence of God? Have you ever been reading your Word and realized that something was touching you and making you feel as though everything was going to be all right? That feeling can't be identified as just "something." That feeling of inspiration, motivation, and power is the authentic presence of God.

I love the presence of God. We know that God is omnipresent. When we declare that God is omnipresent, it means that God has the ability to be everywhere at the same time. How can we even imagine that? A person could never draw what God looks like. How can you draw an image of someone who is everywhere at once? That's something we can't even understand with our natural minds. It takes supernatural thinking to be able to appreciate God's omnipresence.

Because God is everywhere at the same time, we can know that He is always with us. David wrote in Psalm 139, "Where shall I go from Your spirit, or where shall I flee from Your presence? If I ascend to heaven, You are there; if I make my bed in Sheol, You are there. If I take the wings of the morning and dwell at the end of the sea, even there Your hand shall guide me" (vv. 7–10). We can never hide from God. We can never run from God. We may try to leave God, but by the time we think we are successfully away from Him, we will quickly find out that He never left us. That's just how amazing God is.

But let's take this thing a step further. Since God is omnipresent, we are all surrounded by Him, but not everyone will recognize His omnipresence. God has given the believer something that goes beyond that. It's called His Shekinah glory. This is the presence of God that manifests itself in our lives. This is the presence of God that you cannot deny. An unbeliever can deny that God is omnipresent, but even an unbeliever will recognize the manifest presence of God. The manifest presence of God is the level of His glory that causes miracles to happen.

I want to encourage you to do yourself a big favor. While you're in your waiting season, stay in the Shekinah glory. Stay in the manifest presence of God. It is in His presence that your healing will take place.

I've prayed for people to be healed in church, I've prayed for people to be healed in hospitals, and I've prayed for people to be healed in their homes. I even had an opportunity to pray for people to be healed on public streets. They all have testified of God's miraculous healing power touching their lives because His manifest presence was with us. It didn't matter where we were.

While you are waiting for your next move, you have an opportunity to live in the authentic manifest presence of God. Don't live in the presence of fear. Don't live in the presence of self-pity. Don't live in the presence of selfish ambition. I'm encouraging you to live in the presence of God. When you're in the presence of God, God heals your body, emotions, heart, and spirit. In His presence there is fullness of joy and life everlasting (Ps. 16:11).

It's an awesome thing to connect with people who love the presence of God. You will notice that at every point in this book I have been encouraging you to connect with strong, loving, godly people—people who love the presence of God. Connection during your waiting season is critical. The Bible tells us that where two or three are gathered in His name, God will be in the midst (Matt. 18:20). It is so important that you connect your faith with that of others who are believing God for healing. Get connected to some folks who love the presence of God.

Don't spend a lot of time with people who don't believe they can experience God's presence, and certainly don't find yourself wasting time with people who take God's presence for granted. You must be around people who want to be in the presence of God and are willing to receive whatever God has for them. It's a good thing to know God, but you can't stop there. You must be hungry enough to pursue His presence like never before.

The Bible says, "Let us come into his presence with thanksgiving; let us make a joyful noise to him with songs of praise!" (Ps. 95:2, ESV). When you enter God's presence with worship and praise, God enters your situation with the power to change it for the better. The presence of God is so powerful that you can't ignore it. The fact that God isn't answering your prayers the way you want Him to doesn't mean He is not present. It doesn't mean God is absent. Trust that God's timing is perfect and His presence is real. The same promise that He made to Joshua He makes to you and me today: He will never leave us or forsake us (Deut. 31:6).

The presence of God is one of the greatest blessings we have. Your healing comes in His presence. Your healing comes when you worship Him. When you magnify the Lord, His hand of healing comes down from heaven and touches you, and you are never the same again. If you want to truly experience the authentic healing power of God, stay in His presence.

MIRACLE BABY

I love reflecting on the amazing things God has done. Some people don't believe the power of God is real. Remember this: some people need to hear your testimony of what the Lord has done to actually believe. I know God is a miracle-working God. As I said before, I've seen God do what we think is impossible. We have to always remember while we are waiting on the Lord that nothing is impossible with God.

Back in 2014 I was preaching at my grandfather's church in upstate New York. My grandfather gave me the opportunity to preach and run the church as associate pastor. I learned so many faith lessons during that season. One of the major experiences came on a very beautiful Sunday morning. I was preaching about faith, and the faith of one of the families in the church was really stirred. The couple had two beautiful daughters and were believing God for a son, but past experience convinced them that they were not able to have any more children. They had lived through multiple miscarriages while attempting to have a third child. Can you imagine? They tried over and over again, and it just wasn't happening. But upon hearing my sermon that Sunday, their faith was charged.

As I closed my message, I asked if there was anyone in the church who was believing God for a mighty miracle. The wife came to the front and said, "Pastor Marcus, can you pray for me and my husband?"

I said, as I always do, "Yes. What is it you are believing for?"

The wife said, "I want to have a son."

My heart began to beat quickly, because I had never prayed for a couple to have a child miraculously. "How long have you been waiting for a child?" I asked.

"It's been a few years now," she answered, "but the sermon you preached today helped me to understand that our wait was worth it and it's time now for a miracle!"

I quickly asked my grandmother to come and assist me with prayer. My grandmother laid hands on the woman's stomach, and I placed my hand on my grandmother's hand. I began to decree and declare that if it be the will of God, this woman would become pregnant with a son. She believed it and received it. The church rejoiced, and we began to wait on God.

About three months later she told the church she was with child. We began to rejoice and praise God. Once again we were able to witness the miraculous power of God. I believe the greatest miracle of this entire story is that this couple did not give up while waiting. They testified to me that though they had been waiting for years to have a son, they never lost their faith in God. They kept believing until God brought forth the miracle they had been waiting for.

Just as God worked a mighty miracle in their lives, He can work a miracle in your life too. Be determined not to give up. Even if it takes a few years, trust God's perfect timing.

As I am writing this book, the miracle baby boy is now two and a half years old. The couple testified in church again, this time about how impressed the children's doctor was with how quickly their miracle baby boy was developing. The medical professionals said he was developing more quickly than most babies. He has an amazing ability to communicate, and he is totally healthy.

So not only did this couple have a miracle baby boy, but they also gave birth to a healthy little genius. When he comes to church now, he can't be still. Sometimes he tries to run up and grab the mic while I'm preaching. I believe God is going to make their miracle baby boy a great preacher one day. He, his parents, and his family have a great testimony. Still, we can't forget about the core element of their faith year: they were willing to wait on God. They won because they waited, and God rewarded them with a precious baby boy. He released their miracle in His perfect time.

Perhaps you're reading this right now and you are waiting for a miracle like this. This testimony is to remind you that nothing is too hard for God. When everybody else says no, remember God can say yes. The healing power of God is so real, it's so active, and it's working for you right now. Be patient and connect your faith with others who believe God as you do.

In due season the woman in this testimony gave birth to a beautiful baby boy. I declare that you are getting ready to give birth to something great! You are going to win, but you first must be willing to wait. While you are waiting, see your waiting time as a development time. This just might be the time that God is staring you in your face, challenging you to truly believe and trust in Him.

Healing Hearts

Healing is not just limited to God restoring health to our physical bodies. Some people assume that every time we declare healing, we're only declaring physical healing. But there are other areas of our lives that can need healing. One place many of us need to experience healing is in our hearts.

There are so many people who can testify to having a broken heart. The good news about having a broken heart is that it hurts because it still works. Our hearts are our most powerful possession. The Bible says that we are to keep our hearts with all diligence, for out of them flow the issues of life (Prov. 4:23). Our hearts are precious, and we are told to guard them diligently. But even still, they can get broken.

Most heartbreak comes as a result of abandonment. You may have had somebody very special leave you at a critical time in life. The love you expected from them was suddenly cut off. You trusted them, but they proved themselves untrustworthy. Perhaps it was a romantic relationship, and you found out that your level of love for them was higher than their level of love for you. That can cause heartbreak. Sometimes even family members treat us in ways we don't expect to be treated. This can break our hearts. Let's not talk about close friends. Sometimes our best friends can become our worst enemies.

The truth of the matter is, heartbreak is real. The better news is that heart healing is real too. We do not have to let the pain of our past heartbreak block God from healing our hearts today.

All three of the examples I just gave you have come from my own life experience. During my waiting season I had to learn the difference between the people who really loved me for me and the people who loved me for my goods. God allowed me to see the people who meant me no good, even family members. But I can tell you this, if a family member treated you badly and you hold on to that grudge, your waiting season will be full of unforgiveness, and you may miss the person God sends into your life to bless you. Don't allow the pain one bad apple caused you keep you from experiencing the blessing of your future.

Some of my closest friends have walked away from me. But through those losses I learned that God would heal my heart and send new friends into my life who would love me for who I am. If you know the pain of lost friendship, I declare that God wants to heal your heart right now; false friendships will not remain hidden from you, nor will they keep you from what God has for you on the other side of the season of waiting. God wants to restore your heart so you will be able to recognize and embrace the real friends He puts in your life.

Romantic relationships are the leading cause of heartbreak in our world. I've had my share of romantic heartbreak. You can fall in love with someone and they never fall in love with you. It hurts when you discover it, but God heals that hurt. Maybe your waiting season is about waiting for your perfect match. In singles conferences all over the world I tell people that while they're waiting for the love of their lives, God could be healing their hearts from the pain of past love relationships. Let God do this work. He may show you that you have lost your ability to love in a healthy way because you were loved the wrong way. Whatever this season reveals, don't allow yourself to have a bowed-down head. Don't give in to self-pity and sadness. Focus on heaven, because that is where your broken heart has been sent to heal.

The truth is that every hurt submitted to God will heal. The Bible says that God makes "everything beautiful in its appropriate time" (Eccles. 3:11). He will heal your body, heart, and mind, and make them all beautiful again. It doesn't matter how much pain you have been through in the past; He will heal and restore you. And while you're waiting for your next big blessing, understand that the biggest blessing is the healing of your heart.

One of the greatest keys to my healing was forgiveness. I had to learn how to forgive people before I could move on and enjoy life 100 percent. For a season it seemed as if blessings were being blocked, and it was because I was holding on to resentment. It wasn't until I came face-to-face with some of the people who had hurt me that I realized I was carrying around unnecessary burdens. After that encounter I decided to pray and ask God to forgive me for being so mean. I knew my behavior wasn't Christlike and I needed to be healed. When I asked God to forgive me, He spoke to me and said, "Have you forgiven them?" I was reminded of Matthew 6:15, which says, "But if you do not forgive men for their sins, neither will your Father forgive your sins." I knew I needed to forgive. Even though the people who hurt me never apologized, I still needed to forgive.

I've learned that forgiving the people who have hurt you doesn't make them right, but it does make you free! Be free, and be completely healed. You are not supposed to carry the weight of yesterday's pain. So as Ephesians 4:32 says, "Be kind one to another, tenderhearted, forgiving one another, just as God in Christ also forgave you." While you're waiting on God, you should be free—free in your mind, free emotionally, and free in your spirit. When I finally forgave, I noticed that I had more joy and more peace, and I was able to deal with others better. Now I can be face-to-face with people who have done me wrong and be kind. I believe that my ability to be kind to them opens the door for me to be blessed. The same will happen for you. Don't resort to anger while you wait. Resentment only adds to the pain of your broken situation.

I'm excited that I can tell the story about how my heart was broken without it ripping my heart open again. My heart has been healed from those experiences because I put my trust in the healing power of God. I'm blessed now because I am healed. Don't ever let the people who didn't treat you right cause you to miss out on the blessing from the One who will treat you right.

RELATIONSHIP HEALING

Many of my online viral videos are about having the right people in your life. I talk a lot about checking your circle. My highest viewed video, which has been viewed by more than fifteen million people, is about not wasting time with the wrong people. Not wasting time has everything to do with the friends we choose and with whom we get into relationships—romantic, professional, friendly, or otherwise. Even though the relationship we have with God is the most important one we can have, followed by the relationship we have with ourselves, our connections with other people are important as well. The relationship you have with yourself is called an intrapersonal relationship. Relationships we have with other people are called interpersonal relationships.

When you reflect on old relationships with family, friends, and significant others, you may think about the relationship storms that have come, and you may feel very lonely as you wait for the wound to be healed. But know that you are not alone. The lonely feeling won't last forever. I reflect on the Word when it says in Ecclesiastes 3:1–3, "To everything there is a season, a time for every purpose under heaven: a time to be born, and a time to die; a time to plant, and a time to uproot what is planted; a time to kill, and a time to heal; a time to break down, and a time to build up." It helps me to know that there is a time for everything in our relational journey. God does heal all kinds of relationships. Perhaps you weren't the best parent you could be to your children. I want to encourage you with this: God can heal that relationship. Sometimes we don't understand how to do things the right way, whether it's being a great parent, spouse, or even friend. Failure is just a reason to get up and try a new approach. We all have made mistakes. We all have done something at some point in time to hurt somebody. During the waiting season leave the door open for restoration.

Perhaps you're waiting for your relationship with your children to improve. Maybe you're waiting for your marriage to get better. Even if a couple is separated and divorce is on the table, God can restore a marriage. God can restore friendships. God can restore the relationship you once had with your church family. There is no relationship that God cannot restore. God can and God wants to heal the relationships that need to be healed.

Unity is a wonderful thing. Most people who are waiting on God's next release in their lives are connected to somebody who is believing God with them. As I mentioned previously, the Bible says where there are two or three gathered in His name, God is in the midst. This proves to me that God is a relationship God. This also lets me know that God wants to heal relationships. He wants us to be unified. He wants us to be connected. He wants us to walk together in love. So that relationship you've been praying for God to heal, I want you to know God can and will do it. There is work God has to do in us before He does the work in our relationships with others, but He has a perfect timing to heal our relationships.

If you develop new relationships or rekindle the flames of an old relationship while you are still in pain and suffering with a broken heart, you can do more damage to that relationship than good. Let God heal you first, and then He can lead you into a blessed relationship. Remember this—great relationships don't just happen. Great relationships take time to develop, and healing them is not an overnight process.

One of the best things you can do while you're waiting for your relationships to be restored is to pray. Ask God to help you with your current relationship situations. Prayer is a way to humble yourself and allow God to come in and do His perfect work. You have to surrender yourself to the Lord and allow Him to clean you up. Seek God for mercy. Allow Him to help you to connect with the right people and to never experience the pain of broken relationships again. Ask God to help you to make the best of each precious relationship you have. While you're waiting, ask God to help you have better conversations when you interact with people. The Lord will improve your character and help you to be more like Him if you ask Him.

FOCUS ON THE HEALING

One of the reasons people don't receive their full healing is that they choose to focus on the pain. Because they refuse to let go of the hurt, they stay in pain. Don't be the person who focuses more on the hurt than on the healing. Instead, stay focused on the healing. I know it seems like a hard thing to do because the healing hasn't taken place yet, but when you focus on your healing, you are practicing your faith. You're focusing on what you desire and not what you have now. You're focusing on your future blessings, which in this case is your healing.

The devil and his demons would love for you to forget about what God has promised concerning your healing. He sends distractions in the form of painful memories to cause you to lose focus on your promised healing. He also sends as a distraction the fear of failing in relationships as you did the last time. Don't agree with the negative voices that are speaking to you. These negative voices are trying to keep you from focusing on your healing.

Focus has everything to do with how much attention you give to something. So let me ask you, how much attention are you giving to your healing? How much attention are you giving your pain? These are the questions you need to answer to determine where you are in your waiting season. Instead of focusing on the bad doctor's reports you received in the past, focus on the good reports that are coming in the future. Don't focus on how relationships have failed or how lonely you feel right now. Focus on how God is going to restore your heart and your relationships.

This may be easier said than done, but one thing I do is pay close attention to what I do when memories of yesterday's problems pop up in my mind. If I realize that I'm dwelling on the pain from my past, I truly practice what I preach and stop focusing on the negative elements of my life, quickly redirecting my focus.

I will go further to say that if healing is what you need— physical, mental, or emotional—focus on the healing elements in your life. Focus on how things are getting better. Focus on your deliverance and your freedom. If you set your focus on your healing, you will find that your healing comes more quickly than you expected. While you are waiting for your breakthrough, focus on the breakthrough. Focus on the miracle.

When I was in elementary school, we used to tease each other by saying, "You are what you eat." Applying this phrase to what we're talking about here, I declare to you that you become what you focus on. If you focus on pain, you become the wounded and hurting. If you focus on sickness, you become the sick. But if you focus on healing, you become the healed. If you focus on the victory, you become victorious. What are you focusing on today while you wait on God? If you're focusing on the wrong things, I challenge you to redirect your focus.

My prayer is that you will focus your attention on your healing and not the hurt. It's one thing to be aware of what you need to be healed from, but it's another thing to dwell on and relive the pain.

Make healing your focus. Regard it as the most interesting and most important part of your waiting season. Be aware that your healing is taking place right now. Even though it hasn't been completed, the process to bring you to a place of total healing has begun.

Pray!

Father God, I declare that I will be healed and made whole in every area of my life. I ask You, Lord, to bring total healing, deliverance, and freedom to my body, my mind, and my heart, in Jesus's name, amen.

Now, Declare!

- By His stripes my physical body is healed from all sickness and disease (Isa. 53:5).

- My heart is healed, and my heartbroken days are over (Ps. 147:3).

- No sickness or unclean spirit has authority over my physical body (Matt. 10:1).

- I will walk in total health and total wholeness every day of my life; no sickness will come near my dwelling (Ps. 91:10).

- I will wait on the full manifestation of my total healing; God will restore health to me and heal me of all my wounds (Jer. 30:17).

Chapter 10

GOD'S TIMING FOR YOUR PROSPERITY

O NE OF THE things that confuses me when I speak with Christians is their ignorance of prosperity. It seems that they believe we are supposed to struggle financially, but this is not what I've come to know as God's best for His children. Struggling may be part of our journey at times, but it is not supposed to be our lifestyle. God created us so that we could have a good life. Why would we call ourselves children of the King and not live like King's kids? Why would the Bible declare that we are a royal priesthood, a chosen generation (1 Pet. 2:9), if we were supposed to live as if the slum is our only option? It's a good thing for children of God to be blessed. Furthermore, we are supposed to rejoice about being blessed beyond measure, above and beyond. The favor of God is on our lives, and that favor should be exemplified in our lifestyle.

Understand that even though we may be waiting on God

to increase His favor in our lives, we are already blessed. Whenever I find myself in the position of waiting on God to work a miracle in my life, I never question whether or not I am blessed. When we choose to be willing and obedient to God, we are blessed in the city and blessed in the field, as it says in Deuteronomy 28:3–6. We are blessed coming in and going out. I believe that we are blessed beyond measure even before we get our prayers answered. That's just how good God is to us.

Prosperity is real. The Bible tells us in 2 Corinthians 9:8, "God is able to make all grace abound toward you, so that you, always having enough of everything, may abound to every good work." The opportunity to experience the best of life is available to you at no cost. Jesus paid the price for you to be prosperous. However, the devil wants you to believe that you are not blessed. He wants you to believe that prosperity is not yours. The devil and his demons would love to convince you that prosperity is just a joke. But we know that the devil is a liar. You have to learn how to ignore those negative voices in your head that try to convince you that you will not prosper. I declare right now that you are prosperous. You are blessed. You have more than enough. The blessings of Abraham are already yours (Gen. 28:4; Gal. 3:14). You are blessed beyond measure.

There was a time in my life when I struggled. I thought prosperity was just a dream that would never come true. Because my family was also struggling, I thought there was a generational curse of poverty on my life. After a while God began to change my circumstances. I worked hard, and Psalm 128:2 came alive to me: "For you shall eat the fruit of the labor of your hands; you will be happy, and it shall be well with you."

I'm telling you this because I know it to be a fact: where you are right now is not where you will be forever. God has a mysterious way of causing your financial situation to change in an instant. You have to believe that the power of God to prosper you is real. You have to believe that prosperity doesn't come in your timing; it comes in God's timing. Know within your heart that God is not finished blessing you yet.

It's funny that when God opens one door, many open doors begin to follow. It's like you get in the flow with this thing called prosperity. It doesn't just flash in front of your eyes and then disappear. It shows up, and if you tap into it and ride the wave God has set before you, that wave lasts a lifetime.

The blessings of God are alive and active. There is nothing fake about prosperity. The wave is real. The devil may try, but when God begins to prosper you, he cannot block what God has already prepared for you. Don't let what you see with your natural eyes cause you to believe the devil is winning and you will never prosper. Don't allow people who have not tapped into the anointing for prosperity convince you that prosperity is not real. There are treasures in heaven right now with your name on them. God is just waiting for His perfect timing to release the highest level of favor meant for your life.

You may get discouraged sometimes, but don't allow it to take precedence over your faith. You walk by faith and not by sight. Faith will cause you to say, "Sooner or later, God is going to release a mighty financial miracle into my life." You will say, "Prosperity is mine, and even though I don't see it, I believe I have it."

Prosperity is not a joke. It's a serious and very real reality that exists in the lives of the children of the King. This prosperity is in your hands. I declare these words every day of my life, and you can begin to say them too: "I declare that with the help of the Lord, everything that I touch prospers."

I know you are waiting on God and it seems as if nothing is happening, but prosperity is real, it exists, and it will happen for you!

THRIVE!

Prosperity is the state of being successful and possessing the ability to thrive in the area of money. I know a lot of people are afraid to talk about money, but money is very important. We need it every day. Unfortunately a lack of money is the cause of most people's problems. Businesses close because of a lack of money. Churches close because of a lack of money. Marriages end and families break up because of money problems. This is why we as believers need to understand how the principle of financial prosperity works. Money is important.

Where you are right now is not where you will be forever.

Most people I talk to are waiting for financial miracles such as job promotions or opportunities to advance their businesses. Maybe you too are waiting for a financial miracle. Let me tell you, God wants you to be successful when it comes to your finances. God wants you to thrive in the area of money. He does not want you to struggle financially. If this is not true, then why would God promise to open up the windows of heaven and pour out blessings for us that we wouldn't have room enough to receive? (See Malachi 3:10.) It doesn't sound as if God wants us to be broke. The Word of God doesn't tell me that God wants us to live in poverty. It reminds us that God wants us to be blessed.

Prosperity isn't only about money, though. It begins with your being successful in the areas of your health, mind, and spirit. When you are healthy and in your right mind, you will be better able to prosper in your finances. And with a strong spirit, you become unstoppable. How can you work hard and do the things necessary to prosper if you're not healthy, in your right mind, and strong in spirit? These are the things necessary for you to be able to step into the pool of prosperity God has for you.

There is an anointing to flourish. When you prosper, you flourish. I talked earlier about growing and developing. To flourish simply means that you are growing and developing in a healthy way. There are a lot of people who are growing and developing the wrong way. They are developing bad habits, moving toward the wrong destinations, connecting with the wrong people, and failing consistently. They don't even realize that they're getting further and further away from experiencing true prosperity.

While you are waiting on God's best for you, I declare that you will not grow in an unhealthy way. You will grow and develop correctly. Prosperity is about flourishing God's way. Don't be a failure because you grow toward the wrong things, but be a success because you move toward the right things. This has everything to do with doing things God's way.

When you are prosperous, it means you have tapped into a wave of unlimited flourishing. It means that you live in continuous increase and abundance. The anointing to multiply the goodness in your life is overflowing. You live a life that consists of more than enough. There's no limit to your success.

When the anointing to flourish is on you, whatever you do will prosper (Ps. 1:3). Whatever you speak shall come to pass. You have a right to be bold or extravagant in your living. A person who is flourishing will attract the attention of the world. I believe that Jesus wants us to attract the attention of the world for the right reasons. The Bible says, "Let your light so shine before men that they may see your good works and glorify your Father who is in heaven" (Matt. 5:16).

God wants us to shine for His glory. You should never want to prosper for your own good. You will be blessed with prosperity, but ultimately God gets all of the glory. If you want to prosper for your own glory, you are growing in the wrong direction. If you want to prosper so you can get the credit and so that people will worship you for what you have, you are developing the wrong attitude.

While you are waiting on God to release the anointing of prosperity over your life, ask God to examine your heart and prepare you for the blessing in such a way that you will never take the glory or the credit for what He has done in your life.

You are developing vigorously because of the hand of God on your life. Prosperity has nothing to do with your own power. Prosperity comes from the Lord. He promised to open the windows of heaven. Heaven is where your treasure lies. Heaven is where your blessing is stored. God simply opens the windows of heaven and releases the blessing to you.

Our source of prosperity rests in God—not in our boss, not in customers, and not in money. God is our source. People who forget that God is the source of their blessing will try other sources. When they do this, they erect a false god before the Lord, and we know that our God is a jealous God.

Don't make the mistake of being so desperate for prosperity that you try to tap into sources outside of God to bring you increase. Those sources will always fail you. You may experience temporary happiness, but that experience will not last long. Trust God today. He is the source of your strength, healing, and increase.

GIVE!

When you are waiting on God's best for you, use the time to do good things, especially if you're waiting for a financial miracle. In Luke 6:38 the Bible tells us to give and we shall receive. If you have been praying for increase, you have to make yourself available to help somebody else increase. You cannot get to the point in your waiting season where you decide that you're not going to give because you're not getting anything right now. Perhaps your season to receive will come when you first enjoy your season to give.

I've learned that one of the best ways to be like God is to be a giver. After all, God gave us His most precious gift,

His Son. When God gave us Jesus, He gave us life and life more abundantly. Jesus said it Himself: "I came that they may have life, and that they may have it more abundantly" (John 10:10). Why would we want to forgo giving, knowing that this is one of the best ways to be like God?

When we give, we don't lose a thing.

In my ministry I believe in sowing and reaping and often encourage believers to sow a seed into good ground and expect a mighty harvest to come in return. There are some people who are convinced that when they sow a seed, they lose that seed. What they don't understand is that giving is not about losing something; giving puts you in the perfect position to be able to receive.

While you're waiting on God to release prosperity in your life, you need to find more opportunities to give. Give to the ministry you are a part of. Give to the people in your life who need help. It's a beautiful feeling when you can help somebody go to the next level. What if the person you help has been waiting on God to bless them and you discover that you are the carrier of their blessing? Here you are, waiting for God to release a miracle in your life, and while you're waiting for your miracle, you become somebody else's miracle. God would be looking at you from heaven, pleased that you chose to walk in obedience to His Word. This is what it is like to be a giver. What you make happen for somebody else, God will make happen for you. When you bless others, the blessings of God rain down on you like never before.

Become an angel investor.

I have lived the life of a giver. When I discovered that giving opens the door for God to release prosperity in our lives, giving became a habit for me. Even when I didn't have much, I still found to way to give and bless somebody. Even if it was just buying a meal for someone, I sought to be a blessing to somebody else, and I knew that as I did, God was going to bless me too.

I think about investors and have compared the types of investing to how we give to God. In the investment world there are venture capital investors, and there are angel investors. The venture capitalists are the investors who only invest if they can get a big return on their money. The angel investors also expect a return at some point, but their main focus is not the money. Their main focus is to see the business thrive. They believe in the owner of the business and his or her mission. They are interested in investing because of what they believe in, not just to get a big paycheck.

As children of God who are waiting on our prosperity, we should be like angel investors. It's not that there's anything wrong with being a venture capital investor, but the angel investor better models the principle of giving that God honors. We don't necessarily need to be looking for a big payday, but we should be giving to see someone else blessed. When we give to our churches or ministries just to see them thrive, we will get a return.

The Bible promises that the Lord will bless those who bless others. In Malachi 3 we find out how God will bless us. In verse 10 God promises to open the windows of heaven and deliver blessings for us that we wouldn't have room enough to receive. Then it says in verse 11 that He will rebuke the devourer for our sake. It goes on to declare that all nations will call us blessed. So there is a return, but our focus should not be on the return. It should be on how we are able to benefit and bless somebody else.

I get excited when I have an opportunity to give, because I know that giving works. I give as often as I can. Whether I'm blessing a family member, friend, church, or organization, I know that giving puts me in the perfect position to prosper.

Do you want to win while you wait on God? Give while you wait. Don't give more than what you have. Don't struggle to give. You don't want to make things worse because you've given too much. Give what you can, but give. There's an old song I used to hear the saints singing in my old church when I was a little boy. The song said, "Give what you have and the Lord will give you more." Also, the apostle Paul said that we should give what we have purposed in our hearts to give, "not grudgingly or out of necessity, for God loves a cheerful giver. God is able to make all grace abound toward you, so that you, always having enough of everything, may abound in every good work" (2 Cor. 9:7–8). In other words, give what you're able to give, and God will bless you real good.

Don't go through this waiting season being stingy and keeping everything to yourself. God cannot fill a full storehouse. It must be emptied out so He can fill it with new things. When you hold on to what you have too long, especially with a selfish and stingy attitude, what you hold on to will turn to spoil. Release blessings on others so God can continue to release blessings on you.

Testify!

I have heard and witnessed so many testimonies of people who have received financial miracles from God. I wish I could share them all. I will share just a few to encourage you in your waiting season, because while you may not have been first in line to testify, I declare that you will be next. You've been waiting for financial increase for quite some time now. God is going to give you victory over your finances, all because you don't mind giving and you don't mind sowing. No matter where you are right now in life, God's financial miracle-working power is available for you.

One day while I was preaching online, I heard the Lord tell me to invite the people to sow a fifty-two-dollar seed. Many people responded to the invitation, and later one woman sent me an e-mail with her testimony. I got so excited when I read it. She said she sowed the fifty-two-dollar seed on a Sunday night. It was almost her last, but she sowed it by faith because she was believing God for increase. On Tuesday she checked the mail, and there was an unexpected $550 check. She was so excited! She knew that God had responded to her obedience to give as He had led her.

A gentleman came to one of my services and said to me, "Pastor Marcus, I want to testify about what the Lord has done for me in the area of my finances." With a look of excitement on my face, I held him by the hand and asked, "What has the Lord done for you?" He said, "One night I was watching you, and you told us to sow a thirty-one-dollar seed, believing that our harvest time was now." Thirty-one dollars wasn't much of a sacrifice for him, he said, so he tripled the seed and gave ninety-three dollars instead. He said that by the end of that same week he was offered a promotion on his job two levels higher than his current position. He got a bigger office, increased benefits, and, of course, an increase in pay. He told me that if he hadn't sowed that seed, believing God for a financial miracle, that opportunity would not have come his way.

My friend, I just want you to know that financial miracles are real and they are happening. I was preaching at my grandfather's church one Sunday morning. The Lord spoke to me and told me to tell the people that it was their week for a financial miracle. In obedience to the Lord I released that word to the people, and they received it by faith. On Wednesday of that week we had Bible study. One of the deacons came up to me and said, "Pastor Marcus, I have a testimony." He told me about how his family needed a new vehicle. He had been waiting for a while and had almost given up, but just that day somebody had given him a new car free of charge. This is proof that financial miracles don't always come in the form of cash. Sometimes your financial miracle will come in the form of exactly what you need.

These are just a few testimonies that have come my way. The power of God has shocked and surprised so many. I believe that God will shock and surprise you too.

As you read these words, I believe the anointing to prosper is getting ready to fall on you. It will open the doors and release what you need, and you will be able to testify of God's provision sooner than you expected. You may still be trying to understand the power behind sowing a seed of faith, but just give it a try. You are like a farmer who plants seeds in the ground and then has to wait before he or she sees the harvest. This book is about knowing how to get through your waiting season successfully. While you wait, sow seed and wait for your harvest to come.

As you reflect on the testimonies I've shared with you, think about this: each testimony came with a waiting season. Your financial miracle may not come when you want it to come, but God will release it at the perfect time. Your timing for a financial miracle is not perfect, but God's timing is.

When people share their testimonies of financial blessings, make sure you always celebrate for them. Get as happy for somebody else's blessing as you would if you were receiving the blessing yourself. Before you know it, you'll be testifying of what God has done for you.

And then don't hesitate to praise God in advance for your blessing. Have faith in God's miracle-working power concerning your finances. He's going to do it. Your time is coming. You will testify of the amazing hand of God on your life and finances. If God did it for somebody else, surely He will work a financial miracle for you!

CONNECT!

You have read this message many times throughout this book: it is one of my core beliefs that connecting with the right people will greatly benefit your life. And I believe it even more when it comes to prosperity. You have to connect yourself with individuals who have the anointing for prosperity on their lives if you want to experience financial miracles. I mentioned earlier in this chapter that there are many people who don't believe in prosperity. Even more significant, there are Christians who don't believe that prosperity is real. You can pray for those people and you can love those people, but while you're waiting for God's perfect timing to release your prosperity, you cannot spend time with nonbelieving people.

People who do not believe in prosperity will never encourage you to be prosperous. They will motivate you to be content with whatever state you're in. On the other hand, people who are prosperous are firm believers that God's best is supposed to be our portion in this life. People who are prosperous are not miserable people, because they are prospering in their health, mind, spirit, and finances. When you connect with people who have this attitude, your attitude will change. The famous saying "birds of a feather flock together" is so true.

When you connect with the right people, they help open doors for you. When you surround yourself with prosperous people, they are able to teach you valuable lessons about how to get to where they are. You don't want to receive advice from people who are not where you want to be, who are satisfied with the struggle.

Waiting can sometimes be miserable, but connecting with prosperous people will help make your wait more enjoyable. Your wait will be filled with lessons that will help push you toward your destiny.

There have been times in my life when I didn't have any friends who were in places I wanted to go. God had a special way of giving me a hunger and thirst to chase after what He wanted for me. I began to go to events and surround myself with people who were in position to teach me. I would not be where I am today if I hadn't gotten up and changed my surroundings.

Don't be afraid to make new friends. When God is about to change your life, He will change your circle of friends. When God is about to elevate you, He will pull you out of your familiar circles. Don't get too comfortable with people who are not hungry for more.

Prosperity has everything to do with more. *Increase* is a keyword as it pertains to prosperity. If you are connected to people who don't want more, they will be upset when they see you prospering. Don't let this faze you. Stay focused on your future. God will place the right people in your life who will help you get to the next level. As we've discussed throughout this book, you'll spend much of the waiting season making changes in your life. Perhaps one of the major changes you need to make is the company you keep.

Get in the company of successful people. Get in the circles of folks who know what it is to go through something and come out miraculously. If you're waiting for God to release a financial miracle, surround yourself with people who love to give. They will motivate you to give. Connect with people who have a testimony about how things weren't always great, but when they trusted God, He brought a breakthrough. They will encourage you to continue to wait on God and trust Him too. There are some wonderful people in the world who want to help you get where God wants you to be.

There are some people in your life right now who are waiting for you to step out and say, "Can you help me?" There are people who are watching you and see your potential. Maybe they don't know what you desire, but if you make your desire known to them, they may be able to help you get closer to your destiny, and you will have opened yourself up to a greater opportunity to be blessed.

Don't hesitate to introduce yourself to new people. I remember visiting a church in Connecticut one Saturday night. It is a megachurch, and the pastor is known all around the world because of his television presence. Hoping that he would give me at least thirty seconds of conversation, I waited for him to come out after the service. Even though I was nervous about meeting him, I stood there and waited. When he finally came out, instead of just giving me a few moments of his time, this pastor gave me his personal cell number and offered to meet me for lunch to talk about my dreams, goals, and visions. This powerful man of God became my friend. I learned so much from him. I gained so much knowledge from him. My life and ministry haven't been the same since.

What happened? I decided to take a leap of faith and connect with somebody who was in a place that I dreamed to be. I went by myself. I didn't ask if any of my friends wanted to come with me. I decided that it was time for change. It was time for me to get around somebody and in an atmosphere that would increase my faith. The man of God I met in Connecticut is prosperous. I needed to connect with him so I would be motivated to prosper too.

I'll say it again: get around the right people. The anointing that is on them will fall on you. You have to be around it to get it. God will place people in your life if you pray and ask Him to do it. He will allow you to be in the right room and catch the attention of the right person, who may be the carrier of your blessing.

PROSPER!

Psalm 35:27 reads, "Let them shout for joy and be glad, who favor my righteous cause; and let them say continually, 'Let the LORD be magnified, who has pleasure in the prosperity of His servant'" (NKJV). When I discovered this scripture, it changed my whole perspective on how much God loves me. Yes, I've known from childhood that Jesus loves me because the Bible tells me so, but when I read this scripture, I realized that God purposely desires to bless me and that His prosperity comes to those who serve Him. Serving—our willingness to do whatever it takes to please God—is the door opener for the favor of God on our lives.

Here is a question for you: Are you waiting and sitting around doing nothing, or are you waiting and working? I'm not talking about your day job. I'm talking about your service to the Lord. Psalm 35:27 reminds us of the power of our service and of God's desire to bless us.

God wants you to prosper.

God is excited about blessing you beyond measure. Based on what we read in Psalm 35:27, you never have to wonder whether or not God wants you to be prosperous. Your wait is preparing you for prosperity.

When I think about the fact that God takes pleasure in our prosperity, I think about how God absolutely enjoys watching us. He is satisfied watching us prosper. I believe God feels happy when He releases the anointing for prosperity in our life. To bring this down to earth, think about how you act when you engage in an activity you really like to do. Don't you look for opportunities to do that thing as often as possible? If it's something you really enjoy, you may never get tired of doing it. That makes me think that if God enjoys releasing prosperity into our lives, then we can be sure that He looks for every opportunity to bless us and that He will never get tired of doing it. He will never get frustrated releasing His blessings over our lives.

Furthermore, I believe that God is captivated when He sees us giving Him all the glory for the blessings that are on our lives. They would say in the old church that when the praises go up, blessings come down. I'd like to take that faith message to another level and say that when our faith goes up, prosperity comes down. This waiting season of your life is a stirring season for your faith. Knowing that God takes pleasure in prospering you should serve as a faith charge. God isn't confused, and God certainly isn't disappointed with the idea of blessing you. He is eager to do it. He's excited about your overflow. Your waiting is not because God doesn't want to prosper you; it's because He is preparing you.

Don't reject the blessings of God.

I remember a time in my life when I did not like it when people would hand me a blessing. People would come to me and say, "Pastor Marcus, here's a gift of love." I would ask, "What is this for? What did I do to deserve this?" They would answer, "You've been a blessing to my life, so now I want to bless you." So many times I missed blessings because I would give the blessing back to the person who was trying to offer me something nice. I didn't want to take anything from people.

Well, one day my grandmother was standing with me while someone was trying to bless me. She heard me tell the person that I did not want to accept the gift. My grandmother immediately corrected me and said, "You cannot reject the blessing. When people bless you, they do it because they want to. They take pleasure in giving you a gift of love. Don't stop them from being blessed because you refuse to receive the gift of love."

Since then I've learned to receive every gift with love, knowing that God would bless the givers. I learned too that God was blessing me in that same moment.

How often do we reject God's blessings? God takes pleasure in blessing us, but I believe He is disappointed when we don't receive His blessings. Do not reject your miracle. Do not reject prosperity. As I mentioned earlier, there are so many people who do not believe prosperity is real. Can you imagine how they make God feel? When they purposefully reject what God wants to do for them, they miss His blessing. Don't miss the blessing. Don't miss your miracle. Don't miss out on being prosperous.

Don't disappoint God by telling him no when He wants to release a yes in your life. God is thrilled about giving you His best. The devil and his demons will work vigorously to convince you that God has forgotten about you. You have to be quick to review those negative voices and declare, "God has not forgotten about me. He is delighted about blessing me."

The only way you will miss out on the prosperity that God has for you is if you try to make prosperity happen in your own timing through your own power. Stay in position. Don't move out of God's presence.

Waiting is not always easy, because we don't know the timing of the Lord. The outpouring could happen at any time. Our main responsibility is to stay in the right position to receive the outpouring when it happens. Knowing that He takes pleasure in prospering us should help us to stay alert and expectant.

God wants to deliver the answers to your prayers, so your waiting time is not a fight between God and you. It's a battle between you and your ability to wait on God the right way. Waiting isn't about time; it's about trust. Remember, patience isn't about how long you can hold out for a thing; it's about how you behave while you wait.

PRAY!

Lord, I pray that You would release prosperity in my life like never before. I ask that You would bless my finances and my business/career. Let good success follow me, in Jesus's name, amen.

NOW, DECLARE!

- The blessings of Abraham are mine (Gal. 3:13–14).

- Goodness and success follow me all of the days of my life (Ps. 20:4, 23:6).

- I honor God with my finances, and He is rebuking the devourer for my sake. No robberies or losses can come my way (Mal. 3:11).

- I delight in the law of the Lord and on it do I meditate day and night. I will be like a tree planted by the water, and everything I touch will prosper (Ps. 1:1–3).

- I know that God takes pleasure in prospering my family and me (Ps. 35:27).

Conclusion

DON'T GIVE UP

As we've journeyed through the pages of this book, I have tried my best to encourage you. The waiting season will not last forever, so don't give up before your breakthrough comes.

I believe one of the reasons so many people give up and lose hope while waiting on God is because they feel that where they are right now is where they are going to be forever. Don't fall into that trap. This waiting season is only temporary. As you are standing between your prayer and the receipt of the answer, remember this: your blessing is worth the wait. Instead of quitting, you should take on the attitude of a winner and keep believing. Hope against hope as Abraham did when God promised him he would be the father of many nations (Rom. 4:18–22). It took twenty-five years for his promised child to arrive, but God brought the blessing into Abraham's life in His perfect timing.

What if you're just one step away from your miracle? I saw a photo some time ago that showed a man digging through a cave. The image revealed that just on the other side of the rocky wall he was digging through was a big pot of gold. The man took one last swing and then gave up, but if he had taken just one more swing, he would have reached his treasure.

This image teaches us a lesson. Sometimes when we feel as though we have been waiting forever, we quit and we miss out on our treasure. Don't miss your blessing because you choose to give up. Be the one who is able to testify that you waited on God's perfect timing and the Lord brought forth your blessing right on time.

I can promise you this—waiting on God isn't always easy, but it's always worth it. Be encouraged. Don't give up. Wait so you can win!

Notes

CHAPTER 2
IT'S ALL ABOUT SEEING WHAT GOD SEES

1.   "Quotation #34212 from Classic Quotes: Antoine de Saint-Exupery," QuotationsPage.com, accessed December 11, 2016, http://www.quotationspage.com/quote/34212.html.

2.   Claire Cook, *Seven Year Switch* (n.p.: Voice, 2010), as quoted on Goodreads.com, "Seven Year Switch Quotes," accessed December 12, 2016, http://www.goodreads.com/work /quotes/8999494-seven-year-switch.

CHAPTER 3
IT'S ALL ABOUT HOW YOU WAIT AND PRAY

1.   *Merriam-Webster Online*, s.v. "fervent," accessed April 3, 2017, https://www.merriam-webster.com/dictionary/fervent.

CHAPTER 4
IT'S ALL ABOUT DISCERNING GOD'S PERFECT WILL

1.   Karen Clark-Sheard, "The Will of God," recorded on *Finally Karen* (Island Records, 1997).

CONNECT WITH US!

CHARISMA HOUSE

(Spiritual Growth)

f Facebook.com/CharismaHouse

🐦 @CharismaHouse

📷 Instagram.com/CharismaHouse

SILOAM

(Health)

📌 Pinterest.com/CharismaHouse

MODERN ENGLISH VERSION

(Bible)

www.mevbible.com